Praise for
Governing the Small School: Strategies for Boards

"Do you serve a small school? For trustees, board chairs, and heads of schools, reading *Governing the Small School: Strategies for Boards* is almost like sitting down to coffee with small schools' best friend Brooke Carroll. In clear and conversational language, you'll be led through strategies and practical tools from respected governance sources as well as Brooke's own extensive experience. She nudges us kindly and persistently toward governance excellence. As a former head of small schools, I would have cherished this gift of a book that can now be in your hands."

MARY MENACHO Executive Director, Independent Schools Association of the Central States (ISACS)

"Brooke's wisdom about small schools and governance has played a critical role in her consulting work with my school. Her experience and deep knowledge are thoughtfully captured in the pages of this book. With clear explanations and constructive questions, *Governing the Small School* will serve as a vital resource for my work and the work of my board."

CHRISTOPHER KIMBERLY Head of School, Friends Meeting School

"A small school almost inevitably grapples with serious constraints and its very survival may be at risk. At the same time, the school can also achieve remarkable educational results if the board leads the way. But what does this mean in practice? Brooke Carroll presents the answer in *Governing the Small School*. This compelling and eminently practical guide is essential reading for trustees and administrators who are committed to building the school they dream of leading."

NORMAN COLB Former Head of School and Current Trustee, Athena Academy

"Governing the Small School: Strategies for Boards is essential reading for independent school trustees and leaders alike. Dr. Carroll takes her years of experience leading and consulting for independent schools and distills it into a thorough, accessible, and thoughtfully organized book. Part informational, part roadmap, part inspirational, *Governing the Small School* will serve as a constant reference as today's school leaders navigate governance issues in the independent school environment."

SEAN SHANNON   Board Chair, Concord Hill School

"While Brooke Carroll has written for the small independent school board, this book is a much needed resource for any school leader, board chair, or board member of a school of any size. In the aftermath of the pandemic and the emerging realities of a VUCA world, small school boards and their leaders require clarity and understanding of their duties in order to be strategic and forward-thinking. Clear and straightforward, *Governing the Small School* is balanced with anecdotes and research. My book has many dogged ear pages that I will turn to time and time again."

ANGELA GARCIA   Head of School, Friends Community School

"There is no more critical topic than governance for an institution's success, and no one knows small schools better than Brooke Carroll. Through lively prose and relatable stories, *Governing the Small School* provides the framework and support for heads, administrators, and trustees to build a bright future for schools and nonprofits of all sizes and types."

CHRIS WILSON   Head of Schools, Sora Schools, and Head of School, Peoria Academy

"In *Governing the Small School*, Dr. Brooke Carroll lays out a blueprint uniquely applicable to boards of small independent schools. This is the kind of resource small schools are always in search of, and it is equally valuable to the newest board member and the most tenured. I look forward to reading it with our whole board of trustees this summer."

GEORGE ZELEZNIK   Head of School, The Crefeld School

GOVERNING
THE
SMALL
SCHOOL

GOVERNING THE SMALL SCHOOL

Strategies for Boards

E. Brooke Carroll, PhD

BOLD STORY PRESS
WASHINGTON, DC

Bold Story Press, Washington, DC 20016
www.boldstorypress.com

First edition published April 2022

Library of Congress Control Number: 2021922612

ISBN: 978-1-954805-20-0 (paperback)
ISBN: 978-1-954805-21-7 (e-book)

Cover and interior design by KP Design
Author photo on back cover by Jennifer Domenick of Love Life Images

Printed in the United States of America
10 9 8 7 6 5 4 3 2 1

This book is for all of the leaders and governors of small schools out there; wearing your many hats, ensuring everyone is seen and known, working daily—well into the evenings, on weekends, over breaks. Your dedication to the education of our students is remarkable, and I want to shine a light on all that you do.

These pages are a result of my gratitude for your efforts.

CONTENTS

FOREWORD

———

A s a former head of school and current independent school trustee and consultant, I often consider this quote from Harvard sociologist David Reisman when I work with boards to implement effective governance practices: The role of the board is to protect the future from the present.

Indeed, the most successful boards don't just make a difference for their schools in the present; they work to ensure their schools' long-term sustainability in an evolving and highly competitive educational landscape. To thrive, schools need strong governance structures that support a healthy board partnership between the head and leadership team. During my tenure as the director of leadership and governance at the National Association of Independent Schools, we conducted a collaborative study with the University of Pennsylvania to examine factors that contribute to leadership sustainability. Not surprisingly, two of the most important factors cited were a strong partnership between head of school and board and board members who understand the parameters of independent school trusteeship. High performing boards do not happen by accident—they require deliberate time and commitment from each trustee to create and support a culture of growth and continuous development.

Independent schools are complex systems, and just because a school is small, does not mean it is any less complex. Brooke Carroll highlights the nuances of small school governance, giving small schools permission to embrace those complexities while allowing trustees to govern and support in meaningful ways. For example, we often hear that independent school boards must focus on strategy without straying into the daily operations of the school. However, Dr. Carroll offers a realistic approach, recognizing that small schools with limited resources must sometimes rely on board members to provide tactical support. As she states, "When board members and administrators understand the difference between governance and operations, have clearly articulated boundaries that are respected, understand which role they are serving at any given time (that is, which "hat" they are wearing), and have clear, frequent communication, the use of board members to support school operations can be successful."

Dr. Carroll uses examples from her own experiences as a head of school, a trustee, and now a consultant. She bridges the gap between theory and practice, and provides trustees with a roadmap and accessible tools, organized according to her **Three Rights Framework**.

The **Right Focus** examines the concepts of fiduciary, strategic, and generative mindsets while differentiating between governance and leadership.

The **Right People** provides a practical guide for building a robust pipeline of diverse trustees, engaging in sound recruitment practices, and for selection, orientation, and support for new board members. The differences between culture and climate through the lens of equity, inclusion, and belonging are also explored.

The **Right Practices** details approaches to the major responsibilities of the board, including goal setting, meeting and committee facilitation, head of school and board evaluations, financial oversight, and the role of the board in school programs and enrollment.

Each of the three points in her framework is discussed in depth with examples, suggestions, and her own experiences. Dr. Carroll concludes each chapter with guiding questions for boards developed to generate reflective discussions and perhaps to ignite a call to action and inquiry.

What I appreciate most about Dr. Carroll is that she champions small schools and is an advocate for implementing governance practices aligned to their specific needs. Even more impressive is that her approach to governance is equally applicable to medium- and big-sized schools. Governing the Small School is a must-read for heads of schools and independent school trustees committed to the growth and development of their boards and to the long-term sustainability of their organizations.

Anne-Marie Balzano, Ed.D
Senior Governance Strategist
Mission & Data

PREFACE

———

My stomach sank as I put down the phone. I felt bewildered and didn't know where to turn. My board chair didn't fully understand the magnitude of the building issues we were facing at my small school, and during our conversation it had become clear that the board wasn't prepared for this seemingly catastrophic problem. I felt the weight of managing the crisis on my shoulders alone. I had only been at the job for about eight months, and as it was my first headship, I still had much to learn. I felt abandoned and without a real partner on my board.

I *loved* my little school. The community was warm and welcoming, the academics were hands-on and engaging, and the building was beautiful—specifically designed for this early childhood and elementary school with lots of light and open spaces. I had accepted this headship position in part because this was the school that I wanted my own children to attend. The board members were supportive—we had great conversations about how well the transition from the founding head to me was going. There were a lot of things to address, of course, but overall, I was definitely basking in the honeymoon period.

It was a frigidly cold Martin Luther King Jr. Day weekend. On Saturday, I brought a friend from my former school and her children to visit my new school. She and I were walking around as the kids raced through the building on a faster-paced tour. My son ran up the stairs and shouted, "Mom, there is water on the floor in the music room!" I'm not sure exactly what I was expecting, but a half inch of water covering the floor was a shock. I opened the closet door and saw water gushing from the sprinkler head. There were no alarms. I called the fire department and a colleague, and we got the water turned off and began cleaning up. My colleague said, "Oh yes, this is what happens when it gets really cold." Apparently, sprinkler heads had broken several times before. Yet no one had thought to tell me about that or tried to prevent it from happening again. They had kicked that can down the road—to me.

I wasn't upset with my current board. They were as bewildered as I was. It was the board of five years prior, the group of folks who knew there was a problem but rather than address the long-term consequences had only focused on fixing their immediate issue. They were the ones who had let me down.

The MLK Jr. Day sprinkler head break was the beginning of a series of building issues I dealt with. And that first one was in January 2008, right as the global economic crisis was ramping up. My small school, which had been handed over to me by the founding head with relatively stable finances and substantial reserves, quickly became unstable as families withdrew from our school because of their own financial uncertainties. It was a herculean feat not to become one of the many small schools that failed and closed during that crisis. The fact that we survived was in large part due to the evolution and growth of the board. The confluence of major building issues and global financial crisis led me to realize several areas where I needed to step up in my leadership, one of which was that I needed to better understand how boards operate effectively to ensure the long-term sustainability and success of schools. This began a ten-plus–year process of learning, practicing, and going through trial and error, which ultimately led me to become a consultant, working with heads and boards of small schools.

In the course of my work, I have encountered small school boards that are very effective. They have active and engaged members who provide diverse perspectives and skills, are disciplined and consistent in conducting their business and work, honestly address the challenging questions that allow them to think and plan for the future, and understand their roles and responsibilities in a way that allows them to focus on effectively governing without overstepping into leadership or operations. These boards enjoy a collaborative, productive relationship with their heads of school, their schools are successful programmatically and financially, and board members are confident that they are making a positive difference in the lives of students and families. This is what every board member wants! And yet, unfortunately, this scenario is not the norm—it is the exception.

This book focuses specifically on small, independent school board governance. It is a product of my work with small schools as a board member, head of school, and now a consultant. I've talked with hundreds of leaders and board members who serve small schools both informally—at meetings, conferences, and over food and drink—and also formally, in workshops I've led and in consulting and coaching engagements. Through these discussions, one message has been clear and consistent: Small schools are different. There are distinct benefits inherent in small schools that make them desirable to families and employees, and there are difficulties and impediments that make leading and governing them challenging.

I wrote this book to provide support and guidance for the many small school board members across the US and abroad who work diligently and passionately for their schools and yet don't fully understand their role as governors. My intention is to celebrate the efforts, hard work, and goodwill of those board members while providing as much specific, targeted, and relevant information about effective governance as possible. However, there is a lot here! I don't expect or advise that boards implement all of the recommendations at once. Rather, identify what is most important for your school now, and then work through the other suggestions over the course of several years. My hope is that this resource will help small school boards hone their focus on the issues that will enable their schools to thrive into the future, create the culture and climate necessary to support their members, and regularly engage in the practices that lead to effective governance.

INTRODUCTION

Governing boards play a critical role in the success (or failure) of private and independent schools. However, there is considerable confusion and misunderstanding about what boards do and how they should operate. There is a lack of information about governance at all levels: in the parent body, among faculty and staff, and even among board members themselves. It is not surprising that folks don't know what boards do, as there is very little in our society that prepares people for nonprofit or private school board service. Board members are volunteers who assume great responsibility, yet are also asked to stay out of the day-to-day operations of the organization. Small schools with limited budgets, limited personnel, and limited time often don't provide sufficient orientation or ongoing training for new board members. And board work has aspects that are highly confidential. In an attempt not to disclose private or sensitive information, there is a tendency to keep everything about boards quiet. As a consequence there is often a mystique, an opaqueness surrounding governance.

As more and more research demonstrates the impact governance has on the ability of heads of schools to accomplish their work (BoardSource 2021) as well as the overall success of a school (Baker, Campbell, Ostroff 2015), it is critical that we focus on ensuring *effective* governance. Maintaining the mystique about governance doesn't serve schools well. We need well-informed, well-trained board members who are able to think and act strategically to ensure that our schools are programmatically and financially stable and can survive and thrive into the future. We need governing boards that have the right people, use the right practices, and actually focus on governance. And we need informed communities that understand the role of a governing board in order to both support the board and appropriately hold them accountable. When everyone understands how a board works, effective governance can be realized.

We need effective boards for our small, independent schools now more than ever. Our educational institutions have become more complex in general, as they are expected to serve as much more than places of academic learning. Our schools are being asked to address social, emotional, and physical well-being as well as to ensure academic growth. Furthermore, parents are involved differently than they were twenty, thirty, and forty years ago and have different desires and expectations of our schools. And we have different stressors than in the past, with the rise of school shootings, increase in youth mental health challenges, and now the experience of a global pandemic. Heads of schools must respond to all of these factors as a daily part of their work. This is a change from the circumstances they faced even twenty years ago. In small schools with lean administrative staffs, heads of schools have had to shoulder the brunt of these new responsibilities. The leaders of our schools have responded heroically to address these widespread changes, and yet for many schools, governance hasn't changed. In order to best support school leaders, as well as the overall school organization, we need the boards of small schools to recognize the vital and evolved role they play in governing and to step into that role with knowledge and skill.

The majority (85.7%) of private schools in the US are small, with fewer than 300 students (Broughman, Kincel, Willinger, and Peterson

2021) and on average, private schools are smaller than public schools; in 2015, the average private school had 166 students and the average public school had 526 students (National Center for Education Statistics n.d.). Small schools are places where students and families feel seen, known, and welcomed as a part of close-knit communities. Parents seek out small schools because of this community feeling, and also because small schools are typically the ones that offer unique curricula and programs and/or educational support for special types of learners.

Yet there is little in the literature and guidance about school leadership and governance that differentiates small schools from larger schools. The typical research report, article, conference workshop, or other best practice advice is one-size-fits-all. And this guidance is heavily based on feedback from larger schools. For example, in an in-depth, comprehensive study of board governance where researchers interviewed heads of schools and board chairs, two of the represented schools had over 1,000 students, two had enrollments in the 900s, one had 645 students and one had 230 students (Baker, Campbell, Ostroff 2015). While much of this guidance does indeed apply to small schools, much of it assumes more resources (financial and/or human) than small schools have and doesn't take into account the challenges small schools face. This can lead small school leaders to disengage and disregard this guidance, as they feel it is not for them and doesn't address their needs. Disengaging from discourse leaves small school leaders isolated and their board members without the professional development that would enable them to be effective governors.

In my work with small schools, the need to help board members better understand their roles and responsibilities has been clear. Small, independent school boards most often consist of current parents who join the boards because they are passionate about supporting their schools, not necessarily because they understand and are passionate about governance. While their enthusiasm and hard work can be greatly beneficial, their lack of knowledge about their board member roles and responsibilities can be problematic. Lack of focus on strategic and visionary issues, combined with overreach into operational affairs—two of the most common problem behaviors of small school boards—can lead to a variety of problems for the school, including insufficient financial foresight and management, disrupted culture, and frequent head of school turnover.

Having spent so much time in the company of small school heads and boards, and hearing their joys and challenges, I strongly believe that small school leaders and governors need specific guidance, support, mentoring, and strategies that are tailored to the circumstances found in small schools. One size does *not* fit all in this arena. By asking small school leaders and governors to retrofit best practice advice to be useful to their schools, we are disrespecting their distinct situations. We aren't seeing them as unique. Furthermore, having to translate guidance to be relevant to their schools is asking them to work harder than others—and they are already working overtime due to the many "hats" that they wear! We need to provide small school leaders and governors with the tools, strategies, and advice they can implement immediately, that is relevant to their situation, and that respects the conditions within which they work.

How do we best support small school board members?

1 We need to talk about governance more. We need to be more transparent about what boards do, and inform everyone in our independent school communities about the role the board plays and the issues the boards are considering.

2 We need better, more complete, and consistently implemented board training to ensure that board members fully understand and can fulfill their roles.

3 We need differentiated guidance that highlights the unique
   context and circumstances found in small schools.

This is not to say we should disregard the general guidance on nonprofit and independent school governance. The associations, consultants,
and other thought leaders around the US and the world who write
about and provide resources for school leaders and governors have much
to say that is relevant and meaningful for *all* schools. For my own learning
and growth, I draw heavily on works published by the National Association of Independent Schools (NAIS), Independent School Management
(ISM), BoardSource, and Standards for Excellence, along with many
others. Furthermore, there is so much to learn from other authors and
thinkers in different fields. I strive here to bring together this information
and examine it through a lens that captures the realities of small schools.

My goals in writing this book are the following:

1 To help small school leaders and board members feel seen,
   respected, and valued for their incredibly hard work and
   the impact they make on the daily lives of students and
   families, faculty and staff, and their wider communities

2 To provide clearly articulated, directly applicable information
   that will enable small school board members to understand
   basic governance principles, roles, and responsibilities

3 To offer specific advice, strategies, and resources regarding
   how to implement governance practices in ways that
   capitalize on the unique benefits of small schools in
   order to address the challenges small schools face

I've divided the chapters into three sections, representing the three
"rights" I believe are necessary for effective governance: the right focus,

the right people, and the right practices. Boards need to focus on governance and to understand how that endeavor differs from leadership and school operations. As they focus on governance, board members need to regularly and systematically think strategically. Regarding the right people, a board is only as good as its members, and it is critical to ensure that boards consist of diverse, engaged, and well-trained individuals. It is equally important to ensure that all board members feel included and welcomed and that the culture and climate of the board is conducive to fully participating members who make well-informed decisions. Finally, there are a number of practices that boards must address to guide their planning and efforts to ensure the best outcomes for their school.

It is my hope that readers will find in this book not only *what* small school board members should do, but also *how* to accomplish effective governance. I've written each chapter first to provide stories and context, next to offer research and expert support, and finally to suggest methods of application. I want readers to be able to use the concepts and practices presented here as soon as possible with their own boards.

I recognize that all this information and guidance may be overwhelming for some board members—there is a lot here! It is not my intention or recommendation that boards address all of these areas at once. Rather, I suggest that they prioritize what would be most beneficial for their schools and make improvements to their boards in a considered way, one area at a time. And remember that change can be hard and it takes time.

Board service is an incredibly important and rewarding endeavor. Board members who are well trained and who fully understand their roles and responsibilities can have a tremendous impact on a school, and especially on a small school. I believe that with the right focus, people, and practices, governance can be a joy.

PART ONE

THE RIGHT FOCUS

1

SMALL SCHOOLS
ARE UNIQUE

Small schools are not "less" by virtue of their size:
they are more.

STUART GRAUER

W hen I became the head of a small independent school of 150 students, I was provided with an amazing opportunity to learn about all the specific systems and processes of running a school. Our administrative staff included a full-time educational director, a full-time office manager, a part-time admissions director, and a part-time bookkeeper. We did not have anyone hired or contracted to maintain the building. Our budget was printed out on an Excel spreadsheet, and budget models were written in pencil. In my first year as head of school, not only did I have to learn the culture, norms, and expectations of leading that particular school, but I needed to develop a new business plan, an admissions plan, and a marketing plan, update the (static) website, create a new logo, update admissions materials, and hire a business manager.

The board was fairly hands off at that point, so I was learning all this mostly on my own. Everyone at the school was enthusiastic and supportive of me, and yet the learning curve was steep.

I didn't fully recognize at the time that my experience as a new head of a small school was unique. In truth, I was just trying to keep my head above water. Over time I came to realize that my counterparts who worked in larger schools had different challenges than I did. For example, larger school heads aren't typically *personally* responsible for maintenance, billing, or admissions process issues. Or another example: My small school was in a fairly rural part of the county. It was common for all kinds of critters to get into the building. I had recently wrangled a black snake out of the basement (which was not my favorite job!) when a friend who was the head of school at a larger institution mentioned that there had been a snake on the elementary school playground that caused quite an uproar. I asked him who had dealt with the snake—was he responsible? Of course not! He had a maintenance staff to do those kinds of things. I am not in any way downplaying the issues that larger school heads confront or the learning curves that new heads of larger schools experience. I am pointing out that in many cases, heads of smaller schools experience different challenges. I believe it is important to highlight these differences in order to identify the ways in which small schools can use their unique strengths to address their unique challenges.

When I set out to find support for my opinion that small schools are different, and that leading and governing small schools requires addressing unique challenges, I was stymied. There has been little research conducted on small schools, so there is little guidance and support regarding how to respond to the unique challenges they face. There is some research that shows the benefits of small schools on student outcomes such as student attitude and behavior (Cotton 1996), academic achievement, attendance (Kuziemko 2006), and graduation rates (Bloom and Unterman 2014). There is the Small Schools

Coalition, primarily powered by small school activist Dr. Stuart Grauer, which promotes the benefits of small schools. The National Small Schools Conference holds an annual gathering of small school practitioners with sessions that focus on issues relevant to small independent schools. And there is the "small schools movement," with founding credits to Deborah Meier, which focuses primarily on reducing public high school size. All of these resources are valuable, but none specifically focuses on how heads of small schools lead or how board members govern.

There is also a lack of agreement about the definition of a small school. I prefer not to categorize small schools based on size of the student body, although I recognize that this is sometimes necessary. My preference is to have schools self-select as being small, based on the feeling in the school. Is there a sense of close-knit, connected community? Does the head know every student's name? Do faculty and staff joke about wearing multiple hats? Does the board fret about being able to balance the budget on a regular basis? If so, you are probably in a small school!

I love this definition from the National Small Schools Conference:

We ask people to define small for their own school. For some it's about a comparison to the other schools in their local market. For others it's about the number of different hats their administrators must wear.

If you find that when you're in a workshop with staff from other schools you have to translate the topic at hand to the scale of your school, you're probably a small school. If you're filling out a survey and laugh a little while writing "1" in every response that asks "how many staff are in your ___ office," you're probably a small school. And last but certainly not least, if your Head of School is #2 on the list to shovel the sidewalks when the one maintenance person can't make the drive on

a snow day, you're probably a small school. (National Small
Schools Conference n.d.)

While I agree with the National Small Schools Conference that
schools should self-define whether they are small, sometimes a number
is needed. These types of feelings about being small are typically found
in schools that have student bodies of fewer than around 250–300.
The Small Schools Coalition, an organization that "advances the interests of small schools . . . the families they serve, and the teachers who
thrive in this optimal educational environment," suggests that under
230 is ideal (Small Schools Coalition. n.d.) The Small Schools Movement states that schools should be no more than 400 students, and
optimally under 200.

Given the dearth of research on small school leadership and governance, my colleague and friend Dr. Valaida Wise and I decided
to conduct a small, qualitative study of our own. We interviewed
12 heads of small independent schools (with student enrollment of
fewer than 275) and asked questions related to their experiences
regarding the leadership and governance of a small school. Our
sample included seven women and five men who led schools in
five states; four were schools for students with special needs; two
schools served lower to high school students; six served lower to
middle school students; and five served middle or high school
only. We were not surprised with the results we found. There was
unanimous response that these heads of schools believed their experiences of leading a small school was different than those of their
counterparts who led larger schools and that, given the unique
challenges of small schools, the way they led their schools was also
unique. We also heard from these heads that they did not believe
that the guidance they received from authorities in school leadership and governance was always applicable to their situation. One
school head said, "I don't go to those conferences anymore—they

aren't talking to me. I mean, what school with our numbers has an Advancement team? I am the team!"

THE DIFFERENCES

Over the course of my work facilitating strategic plans, board professional development, and head of school searches with small schools, I've had the opportunity to lead focus groups and conduct surveys with hundreds of parents and school personnel about what they love about their school and about the challenges they experience. What is different about a small school? The differences all revolve around the small numbers—there are fewer people in the entire community: fewer parents, fewer teachers, fewer administrators, and often, fewer board members. Schools are small for a variety of reasons: Some are intentionally small to support their mission and/or philosophy; some are new and growing through a small phase; and some are struggling and are unable to grow. Regardless of why they are small, the small numbers in these schools result in two main commonalities: a close-knit community where everyone is known, and scarcity of resources. The close-knit, family-like environment is what members of a small school community typically love, and the limited resources is what they usually dislike. When we look at these two characteristics, we can see that there are benefits and challenges to each.

CLOSE-KNIT COMMUNITY

Whenever I ask parents and teachers to talk about the strength of their small school, they almost always lead with some variation of "This place feels like home," "There is a family-feeling here," or "We are a close-knit community." They go on to say, "My child is known here," and "There is individualized support." These feelings are important, as studies show that a feeling of belonging is foundational to a sense of well-being and can impact emotional as well as physical health (Brower

2021; Michalski et. al. 2020; Ross 2002). While larger schools can certainly create communities where students, families, and faculty and staff feel like they belong, the unique nature of small schools is that everyone is well-known by the majority, if not all, of the community. This provides the opportunity for students to make connections with other students across grade levels, other teachers outside of their classrooms, and with administrators, including the head of school. In a school of under about 250 students, the head of school and other administrators are able to know every student's name. They know the student's family members and a little about their interests and experiences. When a student is greeted by name, on a frequent basis by school leaders, they feel seen and responded to as an individual. They get the message that they matter. This promotes the sense that the student belongs in the whole community, not just in their own classroom.

Of course, students can feel like outsiders even in small schools. Yet because of the small numbers of students, small schools are better able to focus on ensuring that each student (and their family) feels seen, heard, and that they belong. And there are numerous reasons to focus on this feeling of belonging. Carissa Romero writes in a 2015 summary of research findings on belonging in schools:

> Students who are confident they belong and are valued
> by their teachers and peers are able to engage more fully
> in learning. They have fewer behavior problems, are more
> open to critical feedback, take greater advantage of learning
> opportunities, build important relationships, and generally
> have more positive attitudes about their classwork and
> teachers. In turn, they are more likely to persevere in the face
> of difficulty and do better in school. (Romero 2015).

Furthermore, The Belonging Project at Stanford states ". . . clear evidence has shown that individuals in distress who feel that they are disconnected and are not part of a larger community ('thwarted belongingness') are especially vulnerable to poor outcomes, including impulsive or self-harmful behavior" (The Belonging Project at Stanford n.d.).

This feeling of being seen, known, and of belonging is important for faculty and staff as well. A recent Harvard Business Review article reported that 40% of workers feel isolated at work, which leads to reduced organizational engagement and commitment (Carr et al. 2019). When our faculty and staff feel valued and included, they are more engaged and committed, which, we expect, leads to better connections with and support of students.

Smaller schools tend also to have smaller class sizes (although some larger schools also have small class sizes). In practical terms, when teachers have fewer students in their classrooms, they are able to provide more individualized support to each student. And while there is not a scientific body of research that is conclusive regarding the "best" or "most effective" classroom size, there is some agreement in the literature that classrooms with twenty or fewer students have better student outcomes than larger classrooms do (Biddle and Berliner 2002; Mathis 2016). With fewer students in classrooms and across the school, leaders can focus on ensuring that students, as well as teachers, feel like they are connected and belong.

SCARCITY

Because there are fewer students in small schools, and therefore fewer tuitions supporting the budgets, most small school administrators feel some element of scarcity of resources—both financial and personnel. The amount of tuition, the number of tuition-paying students, and the net-tuition revenue are the cornerstones of an independent school's income (the exception being those tuition-free independent schools that are funded solely through philanthropy or grants). All schools must make careful considerations about tuition setting, taking into account operational costs as well as their market's ability to pay. Several factors go into tuition setting: type of programming (with specialized services often able to charge more), type of offering (more amenities can cost more), reputation and prestige, competition, local economy, etc. Yet regardless of what the tuition is at a small school, there are fewer paying customers.

Many small schools struggle to make ends meet with limited income. Careful planning is required, with little room for error. Materials and other educational resources may need to be limited; building maintenance sometimes needs to be deferred; financial aid budgets might need to be adjusted. Furthermore, it is challenging to hire the best teachers if school leaders are not able to offer competitive salaries and benefits. And in a small school, minor fluctuations in enrollment and income can make a big difference.

Yet there are some benefits to having a limited budget as well. Finances are less complicated and creating budgets is less involved. Forecasting is simplified and reporting is streamlined. In addition, there is often a sense of creativity and collaboration found in groups that operate with limited funds. Teachers and administrators must be resourceful and inventive. Pooling resources becomes necessary, which can increase collaboration. There is a greater sense of importance and gratitude placed on what is available, and resources are less likely to be taken for granted. While teachers may long for an abundance of resources, it is important to recognize that there are some benefits to being financially limited as well.

MANY HATS

Small budgets also mean staffing decisions must be carefully made, as salaries and benefits are always the largest percentage of a school's costs. Teachers carry out the school's mission daily, and directly impact the school's ability to function. Therefore, schools typically prioritize teaching staff and must ensure that there is appropriate staffing of all classrooms and programming. Often this means that they must keep the administration team lean. While the same administrative work needs to be accomplished in a small school as in a large school (including admissions, development, business management, curriculum oversight, faculty management, student management, building management, and so on), there are frequently fewer people in a small school to accomplish the work. With fewer people to do the work, each person needs to take on more responsibility.

The well-known adage is that at a small school, everyone wears many hats. This is sometimes said with chagrin, sometimes with glee, and reflects the fact that characteristics of small schools are both benefits and challenges. Two of the main challenges that individuals face when they take on a variety of roles and responsibilities are burnout and lack of expertise. Asking people to do too much can leave them feeling overworked, stressed, and unbalanced. This in turn can impact overall morale, productivity, and culture. In addition, when one person is asked to do the job of many (for example, the admissions director may also be in charge of marketing and communications), some of the jobs may not be in their area of expertise. The result is you have people who are knowledgeable about a wide variety of areas without folks who have deep knowledge in one. The phenomenon of administrators who serve several roles and who feel overworked is a common one in small schools.

Nonetheless, there are also benefits to having a lean administrative staff that wears many hats. Communication can be streamlined when there are fewer people with whom to communicate. This can mean that decisions are more easily made, because there aren't layers of staff that each need to participate. And this can lead to a nimbleness and responsiveness when innovating or course-correcting, a phenomenon that we often see in small schools. With the ability to make thoughtful yet quick decisions, small schools can respond to individuals, opportunities, and crises with speed. While taking on the roles and responsibilities of more than one job title can be overwhelming, it can also lead to synergy for the school and professional growth for the individual. When I was the head of a small school, I used to joke that whereas in another school, a task might be given to the assistant to the associate admissions director, in my school, I wore all three of those hats: admissions director, associate director, and assistant! As head of school, I learned about and was aware of every aspect of our school. When we finally were able to get a full-time admissions director, I worked closely with that person and was able to contribute to every step in the process because I had learned a tremendous amount about the nuances of the position.

It is important to note that there are many intentionally small schools that do not feel significantly constrained by a lack of resources. These schools have developed budget models that are sustainable and fully meet the needs of their communities—including providing sufficient and competitive salaries and benefits, maintaining facilities, and supporting marketing, development, communications, and the overall programs. Small schools such as these enjoy all the benefits of a small school without many of the challenges.

This is what all small schools can strive for: developing a budget model that supports their mission by capitalizing on the benefits of their small size without feeling the constraints of limited resources. How? The process starts with good governance. The most successful small schools I know of have boards that understand their role as governors, ensure they have the right people engaged to make the best decisions, collaborate closely with their heads of school, and plan strategically to accomplish all levels of their work. These boards are disciplined and intentional about what they do and how they do it. They are fully informed about their school's financial and programmatic situations and use data to make decisions that align with their missions. These small schools thrive because they have boards that are strategic.

QUESTIONS TO ASK YOUR BOARD

Why is our school the size it is now? Is this size intentional?

What would change if our school either increased or decreased in size? What would be gained; what would be lost?

What are the benefits of our current size? Think about communication, professional development, nimbleness, culture and climate, individualized learning, etc.

What are our school's major challenges with its current size?

What benefits of our small school board might we capitalize on as we conduct our work?

2

SCHOOL GOVERNANCE
& LEADERSHIP

Governance is not a set of rules or an activity, but a process;
the process of governance is not based on control, but on coordination;
it involves both public and private sectors;
it is not a formal institution, but continuing interaction.

YU KEPING, *GOVERNANCE AND GOOD GOVERNANCE:*
A NEW FRAMEWORK FOR POLITICAL ANALYSIS

I had recently moved back to my home state with my young family and had a part-time job that allowed me the time to reconnect with family and friends. A former high school teacher of mine called out of the blue and asked me to lunch. I was surprised and intrigued because we had not been close previously and had never done anything socially together before. As I enjoy going out to eat, I of course accepted. We had a lovely chat and caught up on each other's lives. About halfway through the meal, he got to the point: Would I consider serving on the board of the small independent school where he was head of school? I was flattered. No one had ever asked me to be on a board before. I didn't even know anyone who was on a board. Board service seemed so important, so unique, so adult! He described the school, its mission and students, how many board meetings they held per year, and the committees I could be on. It seemed interesting and something I could fit into my schedule, so, although I really had no idea what I was signing up for, I said yes.

Over the course of the next several years as a trustee and then the chair of that board, I learned a lot. Our little school went through an accreditation process, strategic planning, and some significant financial highs and lows. Through it all, the board met regularly, had deep discussions, and made decisions the best we could. I don't recall much professional development regarding our work as a board, nor much discussion about our efficacy. We just did what we thought was best without much reflection. Were we effective and successful? In the end, no. Several years after I left the board, when the financial crisis of 2008 hit, the school suffered and eventually closed. Although this was after I had left the board, I still carry with me a small piece of guilt. Did our lack of understanding about effective board governance play a part in the closure of that school? Could I have done more to prevent its failure?

More recently, I was talking with an aspiring independent school leader, an assistant head who had been working in schools for over a decade. I was encouraging her to join a board to develop skills and understandings that will expand her expertise in school leadership. I told her that I believe board experience is a critical aspect of leadership preparation, one that is overlooked in most aspiring leader programs. She asked me, "Who is this nebulous group and what are they doing up there in the clouds?" This woman's work was directly impacted by the activities (or lack thereof) of her board, and yet she had little knowledge of what boards do. I am consistently reminded of the need for all members of school communities, and especially board members themselves, to understand the role of a board and the practices of effective governance.

Private, independent school governance is unique, and unlike anything else most of us do in our everyday lives. Board governance is complex, asks us to take a different view of leadership, and requires a different set of skills and practices than we are accustomed to employing. Here are some of the ways nonprofit/school governance is unique:

1 Board members have a tremendous amount of legal, financial, and social responsibility for our schools. Yet they are volunteers.

2 While board members have great responsibility, they are asked to stay out of the daily operations. Responsibilities and influence reside in high-level discernment, problem-framing, and policy-making.

3 Board members are asked to operate and make decisions *only* as a group.

4 Much of governance work is highly sensitive, and there is a need to balance transparency and confidentiality.

5 Few people outside of the board understand its roles and responsibilities. There are misconceptions and misunderstandings about what board members do.

Given all these unique characteristics, and the fact that most people don't fully understand what boards do, board members typically enter board service with little life experience in governance. And unfortunately, there is often insufficient on-the-job training. While many boards provide some orientation activities, a thorough discussion of board roles and responsibilities and of the expectations and norms of the current board rarely takes place. Board members are left to learn by observation, often of other board members who don't have a firm grasp of the complexities of governance themselves.

People join school boards because they care about the organization. They are doers, volunteers, people of action who like to get
things done. They want to feel like they are making a difference
and to see the results of their work. However, the true work of governance focuses on the long-term and is not always immediately
visible: ensuring vision and viability, thinking, discussing, and planning strategically, and holding leaders accountable. Yet many board
members spend their time fixating on immediate school issues
that appear urgent. For example, when considering current enrollment issues, it is easy to engage in problem-solving regarding
marketing efforts and personnel. These topics are in the realm of
the kinds of decisions we make in our everyday lives, and board
members typically understand how to address these issues. In an
attempt to do something they feel is relevant, and in the absence
of good training about how to engage in generative and strategic
work, board members often succumb to focusing on what is easy,
immediate, and known, and ignore their important and necessary
long-term and strategic governance responsibilities.

Board members who do not understand their roles can be problematic. At best, they are ineffective, and spend their time engaged
in work that has little impact on their schools. At worst, they are
inappropriately involved, meddlesome, misguided, and have the
potential to disrupt the school and board culture, cause the turnover of leadership, and, as happened to the school I mentioned at
the beginning of this chapter, potentially result in the failure and
closure of a school. As the job of leading schools becomes more
complex and involved, the role of boards in governing schools is
becoming more critical. Boards have a significant and direct impact
on the stability, efficacy, and success of schools. It is therefore imperative that boards consist of members who are well-educated, have
a deep understanding of governance, and are skilled at performing
their duties.

GOVERNANCE VS. LEADERSHIP

Governance and leadership are two different activities. While they both focus on ensuring the success of an organization, they employ different skills, perspectives, and mindsets. In general, leaders oversee the day-to-day running of the organization; they manage operations. Governors hold the leaders accountable and, through foresight and planning, ensure the long-term sustainability of the organization. There is quite a lot of guidance and advice about leadership and how leaders in different business sectors need to think and act to be effective, inspiring, and successful. We can find myriad articles highlighting the five, seven, or thirteen qualities, mindsets, or habits of effective leaders. However, there is much less guidance and advice about how to carry out the responsibilities of a board governor.

Just as there are leaders who manage different types of organizations, there are boards that provide governance for various types of organizations. There are corporate boards that oversee large Fortune 500 companies and smaller businesses; nonprofit boards that oversee charitable organizations of all sizes; public school boards; and private school boards. Each of these types of boards has a different focus, set of rules and expectations to abide by, and influence from the norms and expectations of their industry.

PUBIC, PRIVATE, INDEPENDENT, AND CHARTER SCHOOLS

Even within school governance there is variation. There are public schools funded by state and local governments that are governed by their locally elected boards of education. There are private schools that do not receive significant amounts of public funding and are financed through tuitions, philanthropy, grants, and/or private capital. Private schools can be governed by a for-profit, a nonprofit, or a religious body. A subset of private schools are independent schools

TABLE 2.1 **SCHOOL FUNDING AND GOVERNANCE**

TYPE OF SCHOOL	FUNDING	GOVERNANCE
Public	Public	Elected board
Private	Private (tuition, philanthropy, grants, private capital)	Depends on organization (religious organization oversight, independent board, individual owner, etc.)
Independent	Private (tuition, philanthropy, grants)	Independent board
Charter	Public and private (grants, philanthropy)	Depends on organization (religious organization oversight, independent board, individual owner, etc.)

that are governed by an independent board and are run as nonprofit organizations. Independent schools are "independent" of any authority, such as the state, a religious body, or an individual owner, other than their board. In between public and private schools are charter schools, which receive primarily public money and are privately governed (by a for-profit, non-profit, or religious body). While the focus of this book is on independent school governance, the ideas and strategies promoted here may be beneficial for other private and charter schools that use a board to govern their schools.

LEGAL AND FIDUCIARY RESPONSIBILITIES

How an independent school is structured and incorporated will determine the majority of the legal requirements for its board. There are legal guidelines established by the state in which each school operates and also by the IRS. The IRS requirements for a nonprofit or 501(c)3 organization include the following:

1 "Organizational documents that provide the framework for
   its governance and management" (individual states may
   also dictate the kind of document and specified content)

2 A minimum number of directors to "make strategic
   and financial decisions for the organization"

3 Governing bodies must "ensure that the organization
   remains in full compliance with all federal, local and state
   legal regulations" (Internal Revenue Service n.d.)

Note that this is not an exhaustive list, and there are other strong
recommendations provided by the IRS, including this: "The Internal
Revenue Service encourages an active and engaged board believing
that it is important to the success of a charity and to its compliance
with applicable tax law requirements. Governing boards should be
composed of persons who are informed and active in overseeing a
charity's operations and finances. . . . Successful governing boards
include individuals who not only are knowledgeable and engaged,
but selected with the organization's needs in mind (e.g. accounting,
finance, compensation, and ethics)" (Internal Revenue Service n.d.).

Nonprofit boards are considered *fiduciaries* of their organization
and are legally bound to uphold fiduciary duties (Barlow 2016). The
term *fiduciary* means, generally, "to hold in trust," and refers to a
person or group that has legal responsibility for the life or assets of
another person or group. As fiduciaries, boards are held to three primary responsibilities, or duties:

- Duty of care (paying attention to, understanding,
  and showing up for the organization)
- Duty of loyalty (the needs of the organization come
  first, and conflict of interest is minimized)

- Duty of obedience (all laws and regulations,
  including bylaws, are followed)

Duty of Care

To fulfill their *duty of care,* board members must actively participate
in the activities of the board, including making decisions on behalf
of the school while using their best judgment; taking reasonable care
of the school by ensuring judicious use of all assets, including facil-
ity, investment funds, people, and reputation; providing oversight for
all activities that advance the school's effectiveness and sustainability;
and maintaining fiscal accountability.

Specifically, they need to take the following actions:

- *Show up* Attend meetings regularly.
- *Be prepared and participate* Read reports,
  ask questions, and share insights.
- *Be knowledgeable about the school* Understand the
  school's mission, programs, strategic goals, strengths
  and weaknesses, and financial standing.

Duty of Loyalty

To fulfill their *duty of loyalty,* each board member must put the interests of the school before their personal and professional interests when
acting on behalf of the organization in a decision-making capacity.

Specifically, they must:

- Discuss and sign conflict of interest statements annually
- Acknowledge and quiet "parent" or "staff" hat
  when acting as a board member
- Acknowledge and address any other personal or business conflicts
- Recuse themself when appropriate

Duty of Obedience

Board members bear the legal responsibility of ensuring that the school complies with the applicable federal, state, and local laws, and adheres to its mission. To fulfill their *duty of obedience*, board members must know and understand their own guidelines and those impacting the operation of their type of organization, as required by their local and state governments.

Specifically, they need to:

• Be knowledgeable about the board; understand
  their roles and responsibilities
• Read and understand their board's bylaws and follow them
• Address potential legal issues

Board members have a right and responsibility to understand their basic legal duties to the organization when they agree to take on the roles of governors. Although fiduciary responsibilities are not the only ones that will be expected of board members, they are the legal ones, those where both individual members and the board as a whole are liable, and therefore critical ones. Ensuring that there is a mechanism for orienting board members to these duties and explaining how they are implemented and upheld in their school will be important for each board.

GOVERNANCE AS LEADERSHIP MODEL

As outlined above, independent school (nonprofit) boards have legal requirements to establish organizing documents (such as bylaws or a constitution), have a minimum number of trustees or directors, follow all federal, local, and state legal regulations, and uphold their duty of care, duty of loyalty, and duty of obedience. However, within these mandates, there is nothing that establishes *how* boards must fulfill these duties. Independent school boards across the US govern in a variety of different ways: some follow a model or set of guidelines; others do not. There are several models of nonprofit governance that attempt to articulate how to effectively govern (for example, the Advisory model, Cooperative model, Management Team model, Cortex Board model, and Competency model). The differences in these models primarily relate to who holds authority for financial, programmatic, and visionary planning and decision-making. Yet none of these models are legally mandated, and this can lead to confusion. Each independent school board must decide for itself how it will organize its governance activities. Nonetheless, boards will likely find it easier and more effective to follow a set of guidelines or a framework for understanding and implementing the practice of governance, established by researchers and educators in the field of governance, rather than going it alone.

The model of governance most frequently promoted for independent school boards (and supported by the National Association of Independent Schools, NAIS) is based on the Carver model (Carver 2006), also known as the Policy model, which has been elaborated on to become the *Governance as Leadership* model (Chait, Ryan, and

FIGURE 2.1 **THE GOVERNANCE AS LEADERSHIP MODEL**

STRATEGIC
FORESIGHT: HOW WILL WE
ACCOMPLISH OUR GOALS?

GENERATIVE
INSIGHT: WHERE ARE
WE GOING AND WHY?

GOVERNANCE
AS LEADERSHIP

FIDUCIARY
OVERSIGHT: WHAT IS GOING ON NOW
THAT WILL IMPACT OUR FUTURE?

Taylor 2005). This model (illustrated in Figure 2.1) encourages a board to consider its governance responsibilities in the realm of three equally important mindsets: fiduciary, strategic, and generative, and leave the operations focus and decision-making to the head of school and administration. The development of this model in the early 2000s changed the way many school boards led, as it articulated clearly how to think about, organize mindsets around, and combine modes of governing. The developers of this model conceptualize the three modes as "mental maps" or mindsets and assert that each is equally important. "Boards govern in three distinct modes. Each mode serves important purposes, and together, the three add up to governance as leadership" (The Pew Fund for Health and Human Services 2007). When boards establish a process for fully engaging in each of these mindsets, they are able to understand their very purpose for governing. This leads to greater engagement, satisfaction, efficacy, and better overall outcomes for the organization.

Fiduciary

The first governance mindset is the *fiduciary* role, as outlined by the laws governing nonprofit boards: that of caretaker, steward of assets, overseer. It is a critical role, and a board's legal responsibilities of duty of care, loyalty, and obedience are reflected in this mode. This is the *oversight* mode, where boards pay attention to the current issues and situations that may impact the school's ability to thrive in the future. Boards need to be aware of and respond to the short-term success of the school financially and programmatically without engaging in direct management. However, many boards *only* operate in this mindset—they only focus on the current situation of their school. When a board spends all of its time in this fiduciary mindset, it abdicates the opportunity and responsibility for looking outward and forward to establish and reach toward a vision and to assess and respond to threats and opportunities.

Strategic

The second governance mindset is the *strategic* one, which focuses on goal-setting, planning, and evaluating data to inform action. While boards can (and should) think strategically about addressing and responding to current issues, their strategic thinking efforts are even more needed when considering longer-term decisions. Strategic thinking is the *foresight* mode in which boards decide how to achieve their goals. It requires widening the lens to consider more than the current situation and also involves seeking out a wide variety of people and perspectives. It requires data sets outside of the school and alternative thinking patterns. To engage in the strategic mindset, boards need to consider not just what questions they ask, but how the questions are developed, what process is used to make decisions, and how diversity of thought is fostered. Chapter 3 provides more information about how to think strategically.

Generative

The third mindset of governance, and the least practiced, is the *generative* one. Here the board generates "(1) insight and understanding about a question, problem, challenge, opportunity, or the environment; and (2) a sense of the organization's identity in order to most effectively respond to the problem or environment, or to seize the opportunity that best reflects what the organization is, how it sees itself, and what it values" (Trower 2013). This is the *insight* mode, where boards engage in big-picture thinking, meaning-making, brainstorming, and issue-framing that should precede any strategic thinking and/or planning.

Many boards struggle to spend significant time thinking and planning strategically and generatively and are unsure how to engage with governance work using these mindsets. They get stuck focusing on oversight rather than foresight, and/or get "caught in the weeds." Furthermore, as groups, and especially as groups tasked with the success and sustainability of beloved organizations, boards have a tendency to charge ahead with problem-solving rather than start with careful problem identification and meaning-making.

Let's go back to the burst sprinkler head scenario that I described in the preface. What mindsets did the previous board use and what might have been done differently? Prior to my arrival, the school had encountered burst pipes during freezing weather several times. Each time the situation was satisfactorily dealt with in the moment as the money was found to fix the pipes and clean up the mess. The board accomplished its fiduciary responsibility by paying attention to the school's issues and ensuring that its current financial situation was stable. What they didn't do was any generative or strategic work. I wish they had spent time in generative discussions where they asked, "What if this happens every year?" "What threats could this issue pose in the future (such as being dropped by the insurance company, or the presence of mold in the walls)?" "Are there any opportunities we should capitalize on regarding this situation?" I wish they had followed up those discussions with strategic thinking such as "What data can we collect that will help us understand why this is happening?" "What options do we have?" And "What actions can we take now that will impact the long-term sustainability of the building and the school?" If my school's previous board had understood how to think in these different ways, perhaps they might have been able to create solutions and make decisions that would have set up the school for greater success.

The Governance as Leadership framework helps us to think of current issues in the context of the two other mindsets (strategic and generative), and reminds us that problem-framing is as important as problem-solving. Effective boards carefully manage themselves so that they spend time understanding the current conditions of the schools (programmatically and financially—their fiduciary responsibility) in order to use that knowledge to spend time thinking about their vision and destination (generative thinking) and then develop the strategies they will employ to most efficiently and effectively achieve their goals (strategic thinking). When boards spend as much time engaged in a process to develop insight, vision, and goals as they do in processes to develop strategies and to oversee operations, they will fully realize their roles as governors who lead.

BOARD RESPONSIBILITIES

As governors, board members have the individual duties of care, loyalty, and obedience, and they also have responsibilities as a group. The following lists whole-board responsibilities and represents a synthesis of the lists of board responsibilities identified by NAIS, BoardSource, and Standards for Excellence.

1   *Take responsibility for the school's mission and purpose* The board creates, regularly reviews, oversees alignment of, and communicates statements of mission, purpose, and/or philosophy.

2   *Select, support, and evaluate the head of school* The board articulates the head of school's responsibilities and undertakes a careful search to find the most qualified individual for the position. The board ensures that the head of school has the personal and professional support needed and that the head of school receives regular performance feedback.

3   *Ensure adequate financial resources and provide financial oversight and foresight* Board members fully understand and regularly monitor the school's financial standing in order to ensure that adequate financial resources are in place for the sustainability of the school. The board ensures that proper financial controls are in place and also plans for the future sustainability of the school.

4 *Ensure effective planning* The board actively engages
in regular strategic thinking as well as in long-range
planning and assists in working toward and monitoring
the achievement of the school's strategic goals.

5 *Ensure the maintenance and health of the board* The board
recruits appropriate candidates for board membership
(to represent a diversity of thought and perspective and to
reflect the community's constituents), fully orients and
trains new members, and periodically and comprehensively
evaluates board member and board group performance.

6 *Monitor and strengthen programs and services*
The board ensures that the programs and services
provided by the school reflect and effectively achieve
its mission. The board does not manage or direct
the programs but oversees their effectiveness.

7 *Ensure legal and ethical integrity* The board adheres
to legal standards and ethical norms and understands
and regularly reviews its own bylaws.

8 *Actively engage in development* The board
takes a leading role in fundraising and developing
ongoing supporters of the school.

This list is helpful in identifying *what* a board needs to do and accomplish, although it does not give guidance on *how* it should accomplish these tasks. It also does not differentiate how small school boards might need to approach these tasks differently than large school boards. It is important for small school boards to be aware of these basic responsibilities, and to reference them as they develop annual goals. This book is written to provide more specific guidance on *how* small school boards can fulfill these responsibilities.

GOVERNANCE THINKING

When I talk with heads and board members of small schools about the need to think generatively and strategically about their schools, they often respond with something like "Yes, I know we are supposed to be planning for the future, but we may not meet our current budget this year and we have to focus on making sure we have enough money to stay open!" For some small schools, it feels like they are always in crisis, having to urgently think and plan how to merely survive, rather than having the ability to focus on how to thrive. The irony is that if their boards could spend time thinking more broadly about their situation and generating possibilities for the future rather than focusing on the current predicament, they might be in a better position. And yet in the absence of a clear process for this type of thinking and planning, they remain stuck focusing on the urgent rather than addressing the important.

The Governance as Leadership model helps us to frame and understand the three mindsets (fiduciary, generative, strategic) that lead to effective governance. Understanding these mindsets is valuable and helpful for board members in fulfilling their roles. And the list of board responsibilities is clear. Yet I note two weaknesses in this and other models: first, that there is little to support *how* to accomplish responsibilities, and second, the lack of acknowledgment that small schools often need to balance the need to support current operations with the need to engage in fiduciary, strategic, and generative thinking. Small school boards, so frequently confronted with shoestring budgets and overworked administrators, often feel pressured to spend their time problem-solving issues of immediate solvency and/or viability. What tools can we provide to help them shift their focus to more generative and strategic thinking?

FIGURE 2.2 **THREE RIGHTS FRAMEWORK**

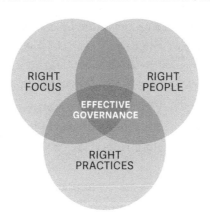

Many small school boards and newly formed boards benefit from assistance in understanding how to lift their focus up from the "weeds" and out into the future—in essence, *how* to think strategically and generatively and *what* to think generatively and strategically about. I designed the three rights framework (Figure 2.2) to guide a board's focus and thinking to ensure they have the right people, the right practices, and the right focus in order to govern effectively. This model, and the steps to achieving each "right" can be used to help boards organize their thinking and planning. This book is structured in alignment with this framework.

The *Right Focus* refers to the Governance as Leadership model. Boards need to balance their fiduciary, strategic, and generative mindsets and engagement. They need to understand the difference between governance and leadership/operations and how they operate in each realm.

These are the steps to achieve the right focus:

1 Understand governance roles and responsibilities
2 Understand governance vs. leadership
   and where and how the two intersect
3 Understand how to think and plan strategically and generatively

The *Right People* refers to the members of the board. Without the diversity of perspective and thought needed to build a robust and productive culture and to engage in rigorous, respectful debate, boards will not be able to effectively focus or make decisions. How those people are identified, recruited, oriented, and supported is discussed in Chapter 4. How to ensure a board culture and climate that supports board membership is discussed in Chapter 5.

Steps to ensure the right members are on your board:

1 Facilitate a bias-free, strategic recruitment process
2 Maintain and cultivate an ever-evolving
   pool of board member prospects
3 Uphold a positive culture and climate, while
   ensuring equity, inclusion, and belonging

The *Right Practices* refers to all the procedures, protocols, structures, and norms that boards engage in to accomplish their work. These include how goals are set, meetings are conducted, minutes are written and shared, and decisions are made. As in all groups, there may be a difference between what expectation is stated and what actual behavior is displayed. Focusing on the right practices helps boards to be disciplined in their actions, and holds board members accountable.

Boards need to maintain effective practices in the following areas:

• Goal-setting
• Facilitating meetings
• Utilizing committees to do the work of the board
• Head support and evaluation
• Oversight of program and enrollment
• Financial foresight
• Development and fundraising

- Board and individual member evaluation
  and professional development
- Crisis management

THE LINE BETWEEN GOVERNANCE
AND OPERATIONS

When I was head of school, I was fortunate to be a part of a Small Schools Association. We were heads of small local schools who gathered monthly to support one another. We met over lunch and had protocols for sharing issues, considering topics, and offering support. One of the most common issues my fellow heads discussed (other than enrollment and finances) was trouble with their boards. And the primary problem was board members who "meddled" in operations in some way. Sometimes the problem was focusing too much in board meetings on operational issues; sometimes it was board members interfering with the head's authority; and sometimes it was board members interacting inappropriately with faculty and staff. I learned a lot from these conversations about how boards should *not* behave and how much stress board members can cause the head of school when they do not understand their role and overreach into operations.

Conversely, I also know from personal experience and talking with other heads that in small schools, board members are sometimes needed to accomplish roles or tasks that are typically considered outside the governance purview. I frequently encounter heads and boards who are sheepish when describing how board members support operations; they know they are not "supposed" to be doing this but feel it is necessary for their school. When board members engage in operations work, it can cause confusion, problems, and even shame. This became clear in conversations with heads of schools through my research on small school leadership and governance. One head summed it up this

way: "So small schools have a hard time with the traditional definition, right? They're supposed to be the visionaries. They're supposed
to . . . stay at the higher level. Well, the fact of the matter is in small
schools everybody's wearing a million hats. I do have board committees doing what in other schools would be a paid staff position."
Another commented on the problems: "So you're inviting them down
from the 30,000-foot perspective into the operational piece and then
you're telling them, OK, now get back up, get back up into the clouds.
That's confusing. And that's a little scary." Rather than pretend that it
doesn't happen, and shame schools when it does happen, the solution
is to acknowledge when board involvement is needed in operations
and establish a process for ensuring that board members engage with
operations intentionally and appropriately. I believe that talking more
about this issue, rather than ignoring it, is what is needed.

Because of their limited resources, many small schools do not have
the personnel to accomplish all of the administrative tasks of the school.
Often, one administrator wears many hats: communications director
as well as marketing director, or business manager as well as admissions

FIGURE 2.3 **THE GOVERNANCE–OPERATIONS LINE**

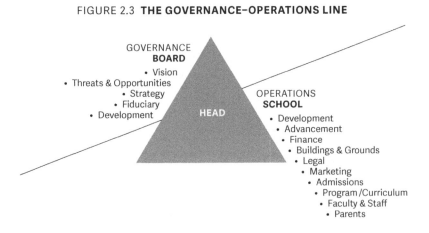

director, and so forth. In these schools, the heads of school may need or want to call upon knowledgeable board members to help out. This is a reasonable and effective use of human resources and can be highly successful, if managed well. When board members and administrators understand the difference between governance and operations, have clearly articulated boundaries that are respected, understand which role they are serving at any given time (that is, which "hat" they are wearing), and have clear, frequent communication, the use of board members to support school operations can be successful.

The governance-operations line graph (Figure 2.3) displays the board's governance focus on the left side of the line: overseeing the vision of the school, protecting against threats and capitalizing on opportunities, fulfilling fiduciary responsibilities, and supporting the development needs of the school. On the right hand side are the operational areas that the head leads and manages. The head sits in the middle and is the conduit between the two realms.

In order to most effectively use board members to support the operations of a school, the head of school needs to be the guardian of the line. The head of school is the one who represents each side to the other and is the only one who is fully aware of the issues and circumstances on either side. The head of school is therefore singularly prepared to manage how the two sides interact. They can let board members know what help is needed and facilitate connections.

There are three ways that board members can effectively support the operations of a school.

1 The first, and most common, is as a consultant or mentor who provides guidance to an administrator. A board member with an accounting background might mentor a school's new Business Manager; a marketing director from another (noncompeting) school or business may provide resources that would help the school's marketing efforts, etc. And

individual board members may be very beneficial in providing knowledge and resources to the head of school. While board members should never be recruited to the board solely for their professional expertise (see Chapter 4), it would be foolish not to use and benefit from their experience.

2 A second way that board members might support the operations of the school is by volunteering. There are myriad opportunities to volunteer, especially in a small school. Board members can support in general ways, such as stuffing envelopes or setting up for an event, or they can engage in activities that recognize their roles as governors, such as making development phone calls or supporting admissions tours. In many schools, this type of board member volunteerism is a requirement of board service and can be very effective. Schools can and should think creatively about what their needs are and how board members might serve as volunteers to effectively get the jobs done.

3 The third way that some board members support the operations of a small school, and by far the least common, is to be unpaid employees. Some small schools are in a position where they are unable to hire the needed staff, and a board member is willing and able to fill the role. This might be data entry, after-school supervision, designing marketing materials, or another administrative task. These roles should be considered temporary, with the goal of hiring paid employees when feasible.

In all three of these cases, when board members serve as mentors, volunteers, or unpaid employees, there are several important things to remember. The first is to recognize that when helping with operations,

TABLE 2.2 **THREE WAYS BOARD MEMBERS MAY SERVE THE SCHOOL**

ADVISOR / MENTOR	Advises head or other administrator in area of expertise	**REMEMBER** • Board members have no individual authority. • As a board member, you have influence. • Board confidentiality must be maintained. • Governance must be the primary focus.
VOLUNTEER	Volunteers at the school	
UNPAID EMPLOYEE	Provides a service that would otherwise require a paid consultant or employee	

the board member is *not* serving in a governance role—they effectively take that hat off. They are helping because they care and want to support the school, not because they are operating as a governor. This is in part because the board speaks as a whole; individual board members do not have the responsibility or the right to speak or decide on behalf of the full board. Therefore, when supporting the operations of the school, board members do not have any authority to direct or correct school staff or community members. They are there only to support.

Conversely, and seemingly contradictorily, the second thing to remember is that even though the board member may think they have taken off their board hat when supporting operations, they will likely still be seen as a governor, with influence and power. School community members do not always fully understand the role that board members play, and this lack of community understanding can cause problems if the board member is not completely clear about the boundaries of their role and the limits of their authority. This is particularly true in the cases of board members serving as mentors to administrators or as unpaid employees. Faculty and staff know that the board is the employer of the head, who is, in turn, their employer. Therefore, many assume that the board has the authority to direct faculty and staff members as well, when this is not the case. An example of this comes from an admissions director friend of mine. She told me that a well-intentioned board member who works in admissions at another (non-competing) school, was telling her about new software that he (the board member) recommended. My friend was confused about whether she needed to implement this new software, as it didn't seem to meet her particular school's needs. But she didn't want to contradict what she thought was a request from a board member, and she wasn't sure who to talk to as she didn't want to break any chains of authority. I encouraged her to ask the head of school to communicate with the board member. The board member responded that he was merely making a suggestion (as is appropriate), not giving a directive. Yet this scenario highlights the confusion that can occur if board members are not explicitly clear when engaging in operations.

The next thing board members need to remember when supporting operations is the importance of confidentiality. Board members are privy to a wide range of information that would be detrimental—or illegal—to share outside of the boardroom. Conversely, board members should not use their privilege to access the school's confidential statistics or financial information (such as family financial information). Even in situations where they are not officially wearing their board "hat," board members need to uphold confidentiality.

Board members must remember that their primary responsibility is to be a governor. If support of school operations takes time and energy away from board responsibilities, this is ultimately not helpful. The school needs active, engaged board participants who have been specifically recruited to serve as governors. Finding mentors, volunteers, and employees is likely easier than finding good board members.

Most importantly, board members must remember that the head of school is in charge of managing the school and needs to be fully aware and supportive of any board member's work in operations. The head of school should be responsible for requesting board member assistance and assigning tasks. It can be confusing for faculty and staff and even undermining to the school leadership if board members insert themselves without the express knowledge and support of the head of school.

A board member's involvement in operations becomes problematic when 1) it takes over or supersedes their governance work, or 2) it negatively impacts the culture or climate within the school or the board. The cure for the first problem is to ensure that each board member understands the difference between governance and operations, and the board chair[1] ensures that the majority of the board's time and focus is on governance matters. Furthermore, when the head of school is communicating with board members about the opportunity for operations support, it is important to be clear about the amount of work that is expected, as well as the time commitment. The cure for the second problem is to have the head of school manage or broker board members' involvement in operations. In addition to establishing the roles and boundaries of involvement, lines of authority will need to be discussed. To whom will the board member be reporting? What decision-making power do they have? How are they expected to engage with other administrators? Discussing these issues in advance will help prevent "stepping on toes" or authority confusion, as well as other problems down the road.

Governance is a different activity from leadership, one that is not as well-known or discussed in our everyday lives. There is much that small school board members can learn from examining leading governance practices, how to distinguish governance from leadership, and how to fulfill governance roles and responsibilities. Small school board members also need to recognize that they *may* need to engage

---

[1] The person elected or appointed to facilitate the group, either the board as a whole or a committee. The term *chair* is most commonly used; the equivalent term *clerk* is typically used in Quaker organizations.

in governance responsibilities in a slightly different manner than their larger school colleagues, such as supporting operations at times, in order to provide the best and most critical support for their schools. To be most effective, and therefore to be able to provide the best possible support for their schools, board members must understand what is required of them and how best to fulfill their responsibilities; they need to know how to ensure they have the right people with the right focus and that they are engaged in the right governance practices.

QUESTIONS TO ASK YOUR BOARD

How do we ensure a shared understanding of governance among our board members?

When do we provide training?

What methods and materials do we use to train board members?

Are board members fully aware of our legal duties and responsibilities?

How do we ensure a shared understanding of the difference between responsibilities of the board and those of the head?

Do we have language to discuss when and how board members appropriately cross the line and to caution when inappropriate crossing is occurring?

Does our board have specific protocols for addressing boundary issues or conflicts with individual trustees should the need arise?

3

———

THINKING
STRATEGICALLY

———

When you think strategically, you lift your head above your
day-to-day work and consider the larger environment in
which you're operating . . . you ensure that every choice you
make and every action you take drive results that matter.

HARVARD BUSINESS REVIEW, *HBR GUIDE TO THINKING STRATEGICALLY*

I was asked to lead a board retreat for a small, struggling, rural, fifteen-year-old school. The board chair had scheduled three hours for the retreat and wanted me to take sixty minutes to talk with the board about roles and responsibilities. As we talked through the issues, she explained that board conversations frequently devolved into arguments and they often ran out of time during meetings. She also revealed that she was worried that the school was not financially stable and the board didn't know how to "fix" it. She said that her board met monthly and that the majority of board members attended each meeting. They were a passionate group, willing to work hard for the school. They often participated in school events, and frequently communicated with the head and other administrators, providing advice and resources. They worked so hard and yet the school still struggled to make ends meet.

The board chair's description of her board sounded familiar, and typical of many small school boards I have encountered. I had an inkling that perhaps this board didn't know how to work strategically, so I asked for the board's most recent meeting agenda. This is the first step in my litmus test about strategic thinking. She sent me an agenda that was basically just an outline; a list of the reports that would be given. (See Figure 7.1 on page 119 for an example of this basic agenda).

I've seen this type of very basic board agenda in many schools. Sometimes they are sent out before the meeting, accompanied by the reports that will be discussed; often they are not. During the meeting, a general conversation about what is going on at the school is held, with the head of school fielding a broad array of topics—whatever occurs to the board members to ask, whatever they are curious about. Some committees may report on what they have done or considered. Often, enrollment is discussed and there is an impromptu brainstorming session where suggestions are given regarding actions to take to "get the word out" in order to increase new applicants. Announcements are made. Yet nothing is truly decided. Overall, board members are passive recipients of information and/or conversationalists who share ideas as they occur to them. There is consideration and discussion without strategy, decision, or action.

I talked with the board chair about the agenda she shared with me and asked her what she hoped to accomplish during the meeting. She was able to list a few of the outcomes she wanted. I pointed out to her that this agenda indicated to me a meeting with little pre planning— what was the purpose of this meeting? What needed to be discussed and decided? How would this particular meeting help this board accomplish their strategic and annual goals? Because board members didn't know ahead of time what the discussions would be about, they couldn't prepare. Not everyone thinks or processes the same way, and so springing topics on board members during a meeting does not set them up to be creative or critical thinkers. I saw her eyes widen as she began to understand. By spending a little time before the meeting thinking through specific goals, and then by structuring the agenda to work toward those goals, she would be able to help her board accomplish so much more. This led us back to talking about the retreat—what were the outcomes she hoped for? How could we provide an experience for the board members that would accomplish those goals? (See Chapter 7 for more on facilitating meetings and Figure 7.2 on page 120 for a more strategic agenda.)

I've worked with many, many boards that are made up of dedicated, hardworking, and intelligent people who meet regularly and discuss intently, share their time, energy, and expertise, and yet accomplish very little. They spend their time considering and discussing without deciding and acting. They may at times think creatively, critically, or deeply, but without a process for clearly articulating their goals and how they will achieve them, they are not thinking strategically. They consider strategic thinking to be an activity that is part of a "strategic planning" process, not a part of their everyday practice. When I point out to boards such as these how they might shift to thinking strategically, it seems so obvious, simple even. Thinking strategically is not a complicated process; it is, however, one that takes discipline. It requires taking time to understand a situation before jumping in and acting, taking time to gather data to inform decision-making, and taking time to make considered decisions. Without the disciplined practice of using data to inform decision-making, boards will struggle to be effective. They will expend their valuable time, energy, and money without seeing the results they expect or desire—most importantly, the success of their school.

When many of us hear the words *strategic thinking* it conjures up the notion of a strategic planning process, one that is time-consuming, labor-intensive, and often exhausting. It is not something we want to implement on an ongoing basis. Yet strategic thinking and what we consider strategic planning are distinct, and need to be considered differently. The process of strategic planning engages a community in setting long-term vision and goals for the school and then crafting the strategies that will enable them to accomplish the vision. It does take significant time and thought to be inclusive and thorough, although it does not need to be exhausting. This type of strategic planning is addressed in Chapter 6. Strategic *thinking* on the other hand, is a process for considering how to achieve shorter-term goals, gathering data to inform decisions, considering options and perspectives, and then deciding upon the best course of action. It is a process that can and should be embedded into every step of a board's work and used at every meeting.

Thinking strategically, or adopting a strategic mindset, means considering and articulating the methods you will employ to make decisions that will help you meet your goals. It includes collecting data and considering options and perspectives when making decisions. "A strategic mindset is a way of thinking that is flexible, creative, research-based, and detail-oriented. A strategic mindset searches for patterns and connections. It is a frame of mind that allows you to drive significant changes in your organization as you articulate your purpose and at the same time anticipate the potential implications of these changes" (Rogen 2018). However, before you can begin to make decisions, you need to articulate what you want to achieve; you must establish what your goals are and why they are the appropriate goals. This type of goal identification is an aspect of generative thinking described in Chapter 2 and supports the board's process of developing vision, identifying outcomes, and articulating success. Goal identification is a separate activity from strategy development, and needs to occur first. How can you determine what strategies you will use if you don't know what you are attempting to accomplish?

In order to be strategic, boards must be disciplined. They must learn and then engage in the practices that they know to be effective. This means they must spend time creating goals for themselves, carefully plan their meeting agendas to include time for strategy and focused decision-making, develop and follow a process for recruiting diverse board members, and engage in the other practices that are needed to effectively govern. Too often I hear board members say things like, "I didn't have time to get the agenda out until the day before the meeting" or "We haven't set our board goals yet this year." Board members need to honestly reflect upon the time that they are spending together and ask, "Was this an effective and efficient use of time?" and "Did we accomplish anything meaningful during our time together?" Board members are busy people who are volunteering their time; wasting it because of poor planning and/or lack of foresight is unacceptable.

SWITCHING OFF AUTOPILOT

In order to be strategic, intentional, and disciplined, board members must switch off autopilot. We live much of our lives on autopilot, moving through our days without thinking very deeply about what we are doing or why we are doing it. This can be a helpful process, allowing us to accomplish the vast array of tasks we encounter each day without taxing our energy and focus (Hamzelou 2017). Imagine if we had to stop and think about every single thing we did each day! Yet this approach makes it easy to allow elements of our day to slip into routine that would be better kept in the forefront of our minds. We all develop habits and routines that may have worked at some point, may have benefited us by streamlining our thinking and our time, yet upon reflection, could use some attention and intention.

Individuals as well as groups can get into routines, and find themselves on autopilot. Boards are no exception. I've encountered many

boards that meet regularly, think deeply, and participate collaboratively, yet never take significant time to think and plan intentionally
about how they accomplish their own work. They fail to set meaningful goals for themselves at the beginning of each year; their
board agendas are basically the same for every meeting; and they get
stuck discussing operational topics rather than strategic ones. These
boards need to set aside time to think strategically about where
they are going, what they hope to accomplish, and how they plan to
accomplish their goals. And they must think strategically about how
to make effective decisions.

DECISION-MAKING

Think about the last time you made a big decision, one that
had the potential to significantly impact your life. How did you
make that decision? Were you systematic in gathering data to inform
your options? Did you carefully weigh the pros and cons of each
option and consider the possible long-term consequences of each?
Or did you make a gut or seat-of-the pants decision? It is estimated
that adults make up to 35,000 decisions each day, and yet we rarely
consider how we make those decisions. Which is fine for the most
part; it would be incredibly cumbersome if we had to stop, think,
and plan before each of those decisions. In a boardroom however—
where the consequences of decisions can impact the very viability
of a school—conscious, careful, and intentional decision-making
is critical.

There is a body of research and knowledge that suggests that the
typical ways groups make decisions may be flawed. Presenting a set of
data (such as finance reports or enrollment trends) in a boardroom,
discussing that data in a large group, and then deciding upon a course
of action can lead to faulty thinking and bias. The research is clear that
all of us have biases based on our experiences, our current knowledge,

and the culture and climate of our group environment. A recent report (Moats, DeNicola, Malone 2021) identified these four most common biases in a boardroom:

- *Authority bias* The tendency to attribute greater accuracy to the opinion of an authority figure (unrelated to its content) and be more influenced by that opinion
- *Groupthink* People conform to the perceived opinions of the majority of the group and dissenting opinions are discouraged
- *Status quo bias* People resist change of any kind
- *Confirmation bias* People gather information to support their currently held opinion or belief

Other biases that can impact boards include:

- *Anchoring bias* People fixate on initial or most recent information and fail to adjust to new information
- *Availability bias* People use only the most readily available information
- *Overconfidence bias* People overestimate how right they are
- *Commitment error* People stick with an opinion or decision even in the face of negative information
- *Stereotype* Cognitive representations of how members of a group are similar to one another and different from members of other groups
- *Prejudice* The attitudes and feelings people have about members of other groups

In order to protect against these and other biases, and to ensure that the best decision is made with the available information, researchers suggest using a clearly understood and consistently used process.

There may be different processes that are used in different situations, yet common steps apply to all. These include the following processes:

- Be clear about the goal and expectation of the decision you are making.
- Prepare your participants before the decision-making in order to allow them time to process and think.
- Establish a positive culture and climate where there is emotional safety.
- Ensure you have the right people to make this particular decision.
- Ensure you have all of the necessary data (facts, opinions, numbers).
- Ensure your group has a shared understanding of the current data.
- Ensure you allow for and facilitate diversity of thought.
- Ensure you allow enough time to make the decision.

DIVERSITY OF THOUGHT

An executive was wrapping up a meeting and asked his group, "OK then, are we all in agreement?" The participants all nodded their heads and affirmed that they agreed. "Well, then, we are not able to make this decision today," he responded. "Think about this and come back next week with some disagreement. Then we will be able to move forward."

A group that always agrees with one another is not demonstrating diversity of thought. They may be succumbing to some of the biases listed above such as groupthink, anchoring bias, authority bias, or confirmation bias. Or participants may not feel that the culture and climate of the group is safe enough for them to offer a differing opinion. Some group facilitators do not invite differing viewpoints, or may actively discourage them. And yet decisions that are a result of robust consideration of multiple perspectives, critical thinking, and healthy debate are shown to be the most productive and beneficial (Motyl 2019). How do we help our board members to use diversity of thought so that we can improve the quality of our decisions?

Diversity of thought, which means considering a topic, decision, or issue from a variety of perspectives, makes sense in the abstract, and yet when we get into group settings such as a boardroom, it is not often intentionally fostered. Purposely facilitating diversity of thought can feel like we are asking for disagreement when most of us work hard to ensure everyone "gets along" and that we all "come to agreement." Disagreement is uncomfortable for many of us, and some try to avoid it at all cost! Yet considering a diverse, or even conflicting, set of perspectives when making an important decision is critical and supports strategic thinking.

Engaging in a decision-making process that intentionally uses diverse perspectives will likely be a new experience for many of your board members. Therefore, board facilitators will need to guide and even instruct board members regarding how to think in different ways. One simple, time-tested framework for this is Edward DeBono's Six Thinking Hats® (The DeBono Group). Board leaders can use this framework to help board members practice thinking flexibly. Alternatively, they can establish scripts or a set of questions they can employ when considering options and decisions, such as:

- How can we think about this differently?
- What are the pros? What are the cons?
- What are the opportunities? What are the threats?
- What might people in our community oppose about this? What might they support?

Considering how a board makes decisions, what processes they use, how they address biases, and how they ensure a diversity of thought is an important step in switching off autopilot and becoming more strategic. The decision-making process is often invisible to people, much like cultural and behavioral norms, and board members may not have had other experiences in examining the way they think. Therefore, effective board leaders will need to intentionally help their board members by spending time learning about these considerations and practicing these skills. Taking board meeting time to consider how the board thinks together and makes decisions will enable them to make better decisions in the future.

STRATEGIZE EVERYTHING

A board member once asked me when his board should think strategically and when to just move ahead with planning and doing. He talked about how much his board needed to accomplish—it seemed inefficient to gather data and consider options over the small things. My response to him was that the most effective boards strategize everything, even the small stuff. Of course, you can't spend *all* of your time thinking strategically. You will need some board meeting time to consider and discuss. Yet over the course of time, you can think and plan carefully about all aspects of your work together as a board will enable you to be most efficient and effective. This means strategizing when you meet, where you meet, how you meet, and what you meet about. It also means scheduling time in each board meeting to engage in strategic thinking before making decisions.

Here is an example of strategizing the small stuff: XYZ school board meets nine times a year, on the second Tuesday of the month from 7:00 to 9:00 p.m. in the school library. They have been doing this for years. Each September, the board chair sends out a list of the scheduled board meetings for the year. There is no discussion about the focus of any of those meetings, whether nine is the right number of meetings needed to accomplish their goals, or whether the time of the meeting continues to be the best for the current group of board members. This board is on autopilot, doing what they have always done without considering their goals and needs for the upcoming year. A more strategic board might consider their annual goals for the year before they schedule any meetings. They then might survey board members to determine the best day and time to meet and the best meeting location. They might think about all of the things they'd like to accomplish and craft a meeting schedule that will allow them to achieve those goals. Strategizing the small stuff means considering all aspects of conducting the business of the board and switching off autopilot to plan for what is needed.

Another example of the need to switch off autopilot and spend time strategizing is in regard to developing the annual budget. In my experience, most boards do a relatively good job of identifying finance committee members who understand the school's finances to some degree. This small group, typically (and hopefully) in collaboration with the head and the business manager, develops a budget for the next year based on all that they know about potential enrollment, upcoming expenses, expected fundraising, and other factors that will impact their financial position. They present this budget to the board, ask for feedback, and then ask the board to vote on the budget. The problem is that the other members of the board who are not on the finance committee frequently don't fully understand the budget and the factors that went into the financial decision-making. They have not considered data or options and can't fully share their perspectives because they don't have the context they need. The board in this case merely acts as a rubber stamp for the finance committee. In order to be more strategic, the finance committee needs to plan earlier in order to prepare the board for a budget discussion. Ensuring that board members have the background knowledge and data they need to consider perspectives and options allows them to make the most strategic decisions. (See Chapter 11 for a more thorough discussion about financial forecasting.) This is just one of many areas where boards need to consider their processes and practices, switch off autopilot, and engage in more strategic thinking.

Strategic thinking is a mindset, one that is important for all boards, yet is especially crucial for small school boards. With limited resources, narrow financial margins, and much work to accomplish by few people, every decision (or lack of decision) has a big impact on a small school. And there are many issues that are both urgent and important in a small school. Boards therefore need to use their time together in the most effective and efficient way possible. When board members think strategically, they take a step back from automation and consider data, options, and possibilities. They use strategic thinking to ask, "What evidence do we have? What are the alternatives? How might we approach this from a different angle? Where are our blind spots?" In a boardroom, strategic thinking is not an exercise to be conducted on special occasions, but a tool with which to consider everything.

STRATEGY

The word *strategy* has been so overused in our society that no one really knows what it means anymore. The origins of the word come from the military and has referred to strength, focus, and winning. In this military context, strategy was differentiated from tactics in that "[s]trategy is how *generally* to achieve a goal while tactics are how *specifically* to achieve a goal." (Horwath 2020) When applied to the business world, the term *strategy* has been used to identify market position or advantage, develop a plan of action, or mobilize resources to achieve a goal. The problem is that the word *strategy* has become confused with the two words it links: goals and actions. Sometimes the word is used to describe the desired outcome (goal) and sometimes it is used to describe the steps that will be taken to achieve the desired outcome (action). It is helpful for boards to think of these terms as describing three distinct activities: 1) goals are what you hope to achieve; 2) strategies are the methods or pathways you will employ to achieve your goals; and 3) actions are the specific steps you will take to carry out your strategies.

Strategic thinking can be distinguished from everyday planning and goal-setting in two ways: strategic thinking 1) uses data, and 2) considers various pathways or possibilities to inform decisions. Many people naturally think strategically and make considered decisions after gathering data and weighing the merits of different options. Others may make more seat-of-the-pants or gut reaction decisions, relying on intuition. Using a seat-of-the-pants method for making decisions works for everyday decisions, yet when acting as a governor on a school board, it is important to ensure that you are thinking, planning, and deciding strategically.

THE 4 × 4 METHOD OF STRATEGIC THINKING

We have now established that boards need to think strategically on a regular basis about how all aspects of their governance work together—both the big stuff and the small stuff. Yet *how* exactly does one think strategically? I've found it helpful to follow a framework to guide my thinking, and use this 4 × 4 method with schools when planning and problem-solving. The first four steps provide the context

TABLE 3.1 **OVERVIEW OF STRATEGIC THINKING**

1 Establish goal/vision	What do we want to accomplish?
2 Develop strategies	How will we accomplish this?
3 Identify action steps	What will we do?
4 Measure your success	How did we do?

TABLE 3.2 **STRATEGIC THINKING STEPS**

1 Analyze your current understanding	What do we think we know? What are our current beliefs?
2 Collect data	What evidence do we have? What data can we collect?
3 Establish options	What are our alternatives?
4 Consider each option from various perspectives	How might this be considered or experienced differently?

and big-picture within which to establish strategic thinking, and the second four steps guide the process of developing strategies.

The first four steps in the 4 × 4 method provide the overview for the strategic thinking and decision-making process.

The second four steps guide the development of strategies which is the second phase of the overview of strategic thinking listed above.

These steps can be used, and the questions can be asked to frame the discussion about just about any decision, issue, problem, or plan. While going through these steps may seem cumbersome at first, with practice it becomes more streamlined and familiar. Boards can use this process to guide the way they consider many (if not most) of the topics on their agenda that need strategic consideration and a decision.

One of the initial ways boards can shift to thinking more strategically is in facilitating meetings and designing meeting agendas, as mentioned at the start of this chapter. There is more information on facilitating meetings in Chapter 7. Here is an example of how a board might begin to think strategically about scheduling meetings for optimal engagement.

Goal: Identify when to schedule your meetings to best meet the needs of your board members and support the most engagement

Strategy:

1 *Analyze* What are board members' current beliefs
  about meetings? What are their expectations?
  What are their practices (for example, do they all
  attend meetings? Do they come on time?)?

2 *Data collection* Conduct a short survey of board members'
  preferences regarding meeting time, day, duration, focus.

3 *Options* Identify several options for day, time, duration.

4 *Perspectives* Evaluate the merits and drawbacks of each
  option, taking care to consider the viewpoints that might
  not be obvious but might impact board members' experience
  at your meetings (for example, board members with
  young children or who observe religious traditions).

The resulting decision about when to hold your meeting, informed by data and having considered different perspectives and options, will likely be a better one than if you had just decided based on what you think you know. Now you can move on to discussing any action steps that are needed (such as informing board members of any changes to the schedule). At the end of the year, you can survey board members again regarding their satisfaction with the new schedule to evaluate if your decisions were effective.

Boards are admonished to think strategically and yet don't always know how to accomplish this or what, actually, to think strategically about. Thinking strategically is not difficult, yet it takes intention, focus, and discipline. Boards that practice thinking strategically, and that strategize all aspects of their governance work, make well-considered decisions that positively impact their schools.

———————

QUESTIONS TO ASK YOUR BOARD

How can we employ strategic thinking on a more regular basis?

What issues or topics would benefit from going through a strategic thinking process?

How can we hold ourselves accountable to spending time each meeting engaged in strategic thinking?

PART TWO

_____

THE RIGHT PEOPLE

4

———

BOARD MEMBERSHIP

———

*Selection of new trustees is a complex process that requires keen
situational awareness, and decisions should be guided by the
strategic plan. Heads of Schools, Board Chairs, and governance
committees must be cognizant of the dispositions and skill sets of
potential trustees and how those characteristics could potentially
enhance or detract from strategic effectiveness of the board.*

BAKER, CAMPBELL, AND OSTROFF, *INDEPENDENT SCHOOL
LEADERSHIP: HEADS, BOARDS, AND STRATEGIC THINKING*

I was leading a visioning session in mid-February with the board
of a small school to help them articulate their goals for the
future of their school as the first step in their strategic planning
process. The board members impressed me—they were knowledgeable about the school and their role as governors, they were
thoughtful and creative in our generative activities, and they
were respectful and playful with one another. It had been a delight-
ful and productive evening. As we sat around the table finishing
up our work, a board member raised her hand and said, "Oh, wait,
just one more thing. The governance committee needs to find more
board members for next year. Does anyone know someone who
would be willing to join our board?" She ended the sentence with
a little laugh and looked around the table. Crickets. Some board

members actually looked away so she couldn't catch their eye. She mumbled something like "OK, we'll keep looking" and everyone got up to go. I was astonished! How could this seemingly thoughtful and strategic board be so thoughtless and random about the way they cultivated and recruited new board members?

If the care and trust of a school are so vastly important and critical to the school's success and even viability, why do so many boards treat the identification and introduction of new members as an afterthought? This is one of the most important tasks a board has: to be self-perpetuating. A board requires a diverse group of engaged, thoughtful, and mission-aligned board members to effectively accomplish its work. The ability to be successful in all other areas rests on the efficacy of its individual members.

And yet, time and time again I see boards that struggle to build the membership they need because they do not approach board member recruitment with the time, attention, and strategy that it requires. I frequently hear that boards only have current or past parents as members because they can't find anyone else. Other boards have no parents, but rather, only friends of the head of school who are disconnected from the everyday life of the school. Many of these boards also struggle to reflect the racial, ethnic, gender, and other diversity of their communities. Current members of these boards have told me they want more diversity on their boards, with people who will be engaged and helpful, yet they just don't know how to find those folks.

Like almost everything else, small schools can build a board with diverse membership if they strategize and then follow a process. When I started as head of my small school, taking over for the founding head, the board was seven people, consisting of friends of the head who met four to five times a year to hear her head of school report. That board provided advice and information, and served as a sounding board for the head of school, yet did very little actual governing. When I left the school nine years later, the board had two current parents, three former parents, an alum of the school, a head from a nearby noncompeting school, a development director from a nearby noncompeting school, and five people who were not connected to the school who brought diverse skills (for example, one was a lawyer and one was a banker). We were able to achieve this diversity of skills and experiences through a planned process of identifying who we needed, who we had, and who would bring balance and expertise to our board.

The board I mentioned at the beginning of this chapter that had asked in an offhand manner if anyone knew of potential board members, was starting at the end of the process and skipping over many critical considerations. Candidate identification should be the *last* step in the recruitment process, not the first. While randomly thinking of people who would be willing to join your board might sometimes produce good board members, it does not ensure you get the *right* people on a consistent basis. Instead, boards need to carefully consider who they need, who they have, and then, who they want. This process takes time. Unfortunately, many boards I have encountered don't spend much time on the process; they leave it to the last minute.

It is typically the Governance Committee or Committee on Trustees (these terms are used interchangeably) that is charged with the work of board recruitment. I've actually had a Governance Committee member tell me that they do not start meeting as a committee until January, as they don't have anything to do until then. Nothing could be further from the truth! First of all, Governance Committees can and should have more to do than just recruitment; they can plan and facilitate board professional development, board leadership succession, and board mentorship, among other tasks (more on this in Chapter 8). In any case, board recruitment, when done well, is a year-round process. And board recruitment requires more than merely looking for folks who provide "time, talent, and treasure" or "wisdom, work, and wealth," as has been the practice in the past. Boards certainly need members who can provide all of these elements, and *all* board members are expected to support the school financially to the best of their ability (as discussed in Chapter 12). The most effective boards, however, use a wider lens when considering potential board members and seek those who add the skills, experiences, and perspectives that will be most beneficial for the school.

This is the schedule the Governance Committee at my school chose to use: Early in the school year (September), the committee surveyed the current board for their self-identification of skills, abilities, and perspectives. The committee presented the summary data to the full board in November, and together we identified what skills, abilities, and perspectives would enhance our board for the coming year based on our current and future goals and the openings we anticipated. Each of our board members was then asked to bring three names to the committee by the January board meeting. They therefore had a couple of months to think about whom they might suggest. With the names generated by the board members, the governance committee had a robust list of people and was then able to begin the process of vetting before the deadline of presenting names of board candidates at the April board meeting. The final vote on new board members took place at our annual meeting in June, and the orientation of new board members started in July.

WHO YOU HAVE, WANT, AND NEED

This cycle of a governance committee's work needs to start with the consideration by the full board about what they want to accomplish in the upcoming years. In other words, the goal setting discussed in Chapter 6 is the basis for the start of the governance committee's work. Each year, boards have slightly different issues to address based on the circumstances and needs of the school. Do you have a strategic planning process coming up that could use someone who has experience in strategic planning? Are you about to enter into a capital campaign or building process? Perhaps you could find board members who have skills that would support those endeavors. Before you start recruiting, understand the tasks for which you are recruiting.

The recruitment of new board members also needs to be grounded by the board's bylaws. Following the written expectations for the number of board members and their term limits is essential to keep your board legally compliant (see below for more on bylaws). Likewise, before you begin asking people to join your board, you need to understand the skills, abilities, and characteristics that would help and support your board. Boards need diversity of perspective, skill, and thought to operate and make decisions most effectively. In order to know who you need to bring on to your board to complement its existing diversity, you need to fully recognize the characteristics of the members who are currently serving on your board. This is best accomplished by asking your board members how they identify and what skills they bring, rather than by guessing. Once you have a clear picture of the members you have, you can plan for who you need.

The board at my small school developed a self-report spreadsheet, based on models from NAIS and ISM to help us identify who we had on our board. It included the basic list of social identifiers: age, race, and gender, along with a long list of skills, abilities, and experiences. We periodically asked board members to fill it out so we had a picture of who was represented on the board and where the "holes" were. We used this as a loose guide to inform us as we looked for potential board members, rather than looking for a specific person with all the characteristics we lacked. I caution boards not to start looking for a particular "avatar," someone who has a specific series of characteristics you seek. Please don't focus on "an Asian American woman aged thirty-five with a marketing background who lives two towns over." This is limiting and perhaps impossible. Rather, consider all the skills, perspectives, and experiences that you would like on your board and then consider where you might find potential board members who will add those characteristics.

Each board can develop their own list of skills, abilities, and perspectives that they desire, and then create a self-report form to identify the characteristics and expertise of current board members (see Appendix 1 for a sample board expertise self-report form). It is important to ensure that board members self-report on this form; do not fill in the information for anyone else. Social identifiers should always be self-reported and board members may have skills and experiences of which you are unaware. Then boards can create a board expertise summary to visually see the skills, abilities and perspectives that are currently represented on the board and those that are lacking (see Appendix 2 for a sample board expertise summary spreadsheet).

When considering who your board needs, there is a tendency to think about who would "fit in." We typically want people who will get along, not make waves, collaborate, and play by our rules. However, this type of thinking, while comfortable, is short-sighted and leads to biased decision-making, both in the vetting process of board member recruitment and ultimately in all boardroom decisions. When we look for people who will "get along" we tend to find people who look, think, and act like us. This process leads to homogeneously configured boards. Instead, the board should think about who will be *additive*[1]; that is, who will add value and perspective to the decisions the board will need to make. These additive people will likely not look, speak, or act exactly like us; nor should they. We know about the power of diversity to improve the decisions and outcomes for a group or organization (see Chapter 3), and ensuring

_____

[1] Credit for the concept of additive board members goes to Dr. Valaida Wise.

that diversity on our boards starts with the ways that we recruit and vet potential board members.

Once you articulate who you want and who you have, you can identify who you need to add to your board and where you might find those people. This step in the process is the one that often stymies boards the most. They think, "Why would anyone outside of our little school want to serve on our board? What is in it for them?" These boards are approaching the recruitment of board members from a charity perspective; pleading with potential members to help their school. I suggest that there are many reasons someone would want to serve on an independent school board, and board recruiters should take a different perspective that offers board member candidates the *opportunity* to serve on their board. When you flip the perspective, it changes the conversation.

There are many reasons someone might want to serve on an independent school board, especially a small school board. As mentioned in Chapter 2, this type of governance is unique and provides an opportunity for people to learn new skills. Board service is *service*—and provides an opportunity for people to give back to their community, to fulfill their civic responsibilities. For local business owners, board service may be a type of marketing or partnership opportunity (although a thin one—potential conflicts of interest need to be addressed). And for aspiring leaders in other schools, board service is a rich opportunity for them to gain key skills that will help them as they grow into leadership roles. Furthermore, in small schools, where community engagement is key and resources are limited, there is both a sense of camaraderie and impact that are not always found in larger school boards. Board service can and should be seen as a respectable, honorable, and important form of service. When board recruiters take this perspective, and approach recruitment by offering opportunities rather than begging for support, it widens the lens on who might be considered a candidate for their board.

With that widened lens, where do small schools look for potential board members? First, of course, is within the current parent body. There are many different thoughts and philosophies about having current parents serve as board members. Some believe that a board should not include any current parents, as it is so difficult for them to be impartial and there are so many potential conflicts of interest. Others believe that having current parents on a board is beneficial, and brings a perspective that is helpful, especially to a small school board. Whatever your board decides is best for your school, make sure you do not *only* have parents on your board. A board with "only" any group (only men, European Americans, parents, and so on) will be a homogeneous group and will not be as effective as a more diverse group. Bringing in outside perspectives will enable you to capitalize on the power of diversity to have better discussions and make better decisions.

The next two constituent groups that can provide beneficial board members are grandparents (or other family members) of current students and alumni (or parents of alumni). People in both of these groups have connections to the school and personal reasons to want to support the school, but have fewer direct connections and potential conflicts of interest. Parents of former students are especially good candidates, as they know the school well and yet don't have "skin in the game."

Beyond people who are closely connected to your school, where do you find others who may be interested in serving on your board? Start with your current board members, head of school, and school administrators and ask them to think creatively about people they know who would bring the identified needed skills, abilities, and perspectives to your board. Ask your current constituents to think about:

- Friends, neighbors, faith community members, and work colleagues

- Local, connected businesses and partners
- Your local chamber of commerce
- Your local service groups such as
  Rotary, Kiwanis, the Lions Club
- Professional service companies such as law firms,
  accounting firms, civil engineering firms, architects
- School personnel in nearby, noncompeting schools

Once you have identified where to find people whom you might recruit for your board, then you need to determine how you will recruit them. What will you say? What materials will you ask them to submit? How will you decide whether to accept them? The process boards use to vet potential board members is very important and is a key step in reducing bias. Bias can occur when decisions are made based on gut reaction and by "bending the rules—just this once." Rather, boards need to create a vetting process that is as objective as possible and then follow it every time. Nonetheless, you must also remember that this vetting process may be the first interaction a potential board member has with your school. You need a process that is positive and welcoming as well as objective, and approach this process as if you are cultivating relationships and "friends of the school" even if they do not become active board members.

When I was head of school, after my board chair and I had improved the process of diversifying our board, I began to hear from board members in their first year that they were not going to stay on our board. They didn't feel that they were contributing enough to be of value. I was frantic. I would hurriedly explain to these folks that they were indeed valuable, that understanding board governance takes time, and that no one expected them to be board leaders in their first year. *"Please,"* I begged, "don't leave!" I finally realized that my problem was that we hadn't effectively oriented these new board members to our board. We hadn't sufficiently informed them of the expectations for board members at our school, how they could contribute, or what board governance entailed. We left them to figure this all out on their own, and to learn from other board members who just barely knew these things themselves.

So we developed a three-part orientation process to inform and train our new board members and to provide ongoing board development for all board members. We began by improving our board handbook to include all of the documents, job descriptions, and other information we believed board members needed. We gave this handbook, along with a guidebook on trusteeship, to all new board members during a new board member orientation meeting. At this meeting with both the board chair and me (head of school), we went through the board handbook, toured the school and talked about school goals and initiatives, went over the mission and vision of the school and the current strategic plan goals and strategies, and facilitated questions. The third step was to revamp our board retreat held every September. We extended it to a full day that included team building, professional development, and goal-setting for the year. Every year at this retreat, we asked each board member to fill out a conflict of interest statement and a board contract that outlined the basic expectations of board service at our school. What we didn't do—the fourth step that I now highly recommend—is to set up a board mentorship program. Intentionally connecting new board members with seasoned board members to provide support is very beneficial. Once we did a better job of orienting new members, to my relief, I stopped having first-year board members ask to leave.

In order for boards to focus most effectively and engage in the right governance practices, they need to have the right people serving as members. This doesn't happen by chance. Boards need a clear, strategic process for identifying, vetting, recruiting, orienting, and supporting their board members. The time, thought, planning, and energy needed for this should be prioritized. All members of the board need to participate and recognize the importance of this work. Below is a summary of the process and considerations for how boards can use the various steps to effectively recruit and onboard diverse board members.

SUMMARY OF THE RECRUITMENT PROCESS

Boards that spend time strategically conducting a board member recruitment process over the course of the year will result in board membership that will best support the school. This process also ensures that board members are fully aware of their expectations and prepared for board service.

1 Be aware of, and adhere to, board member requirements in your bylaws.
2 Identify the long-range and annual goals of the board and the school in order to identify the skills needed to accomplish them.
3 Consider the talents, skills, and perspectives already present on the board.
4 Identify the types of people, skills, and perspectives that would add to the board.
5 Identify where to find people who would add to the board.
6 Follow a process for vetting that eliminates discrimination and bias and also establishes prospective board members as friends of the school.
7 Follow an orientation process that effectively welcomes and includes new board members in the culture and expectations of the board.

NUMBERS, BYLAWS, TERM LIMITS, AND JOB DESCRIPTIONS

A strategic process for ensuring an effective, diverse board starts with written documentation, including bylaws (reviewed and approved by an attorney who is knowledgeable about independent schools) and job descriptions. The bylaws should state the minimum and maximum number of board members required to serve on the board. Typically, this is somewhere between five and twenty members. A recent NAIS Governance Study (NAIS 2018) showed that the average number of board members for NAIS schools was nineteen, down from twenty-one in 2012, and twenty-two in 2006. Schools need to consider how many board members they need to conduct the work of their committees and boards, while maintaining a number that allows for meaningful discussions when all together.

Research on group efficacy indicates that groups of four to six are most conducive to full participation and productive decision-making (Gurteen n.d.). This is why much of the work of a board is conducted within its committees; it is easier for everyone to participate (see Chapter 8). Effective boards use their committees for deep discernment, followed by recommendations to the full board for final consideration and decision-making. If a board has three to four standing committees of four people in each, and only asks board members (other than the board chair) to serve on one committee, then it needs twelve to sixteen board members.

A board's bylaws also identify term limits for board members. There is no legal requirement for a board to have term limits for board members, and some boards do not have them. Board members can stay on these boards for as long as they like and often do so, even for decades. This works for some schools that claim that the institutional knowledge they enjoy with long-serving board members is a significant benefit. However, many school leaders believe that enforcing term limits for board members is the overall best practice. Term limits enable new perspectives to be added regularly to a board and prevent individuals from becoming too influential over time. And even with term limits, board members can serve for a significant amount of time. Many boards have member terms of three years that can be renewed up to three times, resulting in service of nine years. Then there are often provisions that board members can be newly elected after stepping off the board for one to two years. Term limits offer the opportunity for reflection about the efficacy of board members and the evolving needs of the board at regular intervals and are therefore recommended.

A job description is an important document that articulates the expectations and responsibilities for board members. It reiterates the requirements identified in the bylaws and begins to establish the expected behaviors that will become norms for the board. Boards can also have job descriptions for the board chair and committee chairs. These documents should be accessed and referred to regularly, to inform the work of the board and to be used by the governance committee as they conduct their work of recruiting and orienting new board members.

THE POWER OF DIVERSITY

As we begin the 2020s in the United States, we are a country grappling with our individual, collective, and societal relationships with racial, ethnic, and gender diversity. Our country's history of structural racism, classism, and sexism has been discussed for decades, and yet we continue to work to understand and reconcile these challenging issues. Many of our private, independent schools, steeped in tradition, struggle to understand how to meaningfully diversify themselves at all levels. This issue is becoming more prominent, and some schools' missteps are making national headlines. Embracing, supporting, and sustaining a wide range of diverse members within our schools has always been important and is currently, in many places, becoming mandatory. The logical place for this to start is at the top, with the board. And yet boardrooms often do not reflect the communities they serve (BoardSource 2021). There are practical, moral, and financial reasons why a board needs to consider its own membership in regards to diversity (as well as equity, inclusion, and belonging, discussed in Chapter 5). Yet these are not always apparent to individual board members, and we know that change does not come easily.

There is a growing body of research that indicates that diverse groups of people make better decisions, stay together longer, are more innovative, have better financial performance, and actually work harder than homogenous groups (Hak 2019; Hayes, 2017; Larson 2017). And we need our boards to be cohesive, work hard, make good and innovative decisions, and produce strong financial outcomes for our schools. Groups are positively impacted by racial, ethnic, gender, age, socioeconomic, cultural, and other types of diversity when, as discussed in Chapter 5, all members feel included, valued, and heard. Therefore it is imperative that independent school boards consider 1) who is on their board and what perspectives they represent (diversity), and 2) how welcomed and included their board members feel (equity, inclusion, belonging). This focus may be new to some board members; it may be uncomfortable, and some board members may be resistant to change. A recent BoardSource study found "boards that are predominantly white are more likely to identify board candidates that are very much like themselves—white individuals who are typically from similar socioeconomic backgrounds with similar lived experiences and perspectives. As long as boards continue to approach board recruitment with this mindset, the lack of diversity in nonprofit leadership is unlikely to change significantly" (BoardSource 2021). Diversifying our boards is work that needs to be done, not only because it is the right thing to do, but because it will produce the best results for our schools.

When considering who would best serve on your board, considering the diversity of background and perspective that is found in your school and wider community (in other words, the diversity of social identifiers such as race, ethnicity, age, and gender) and ensuring that your board reflects this diversity, is the first step. There are a variety of books and articles that consider our nation's history of racism, classism, and sexism, and provide context and suggestions for moving toward becoming more equitable and just communities. Learning from these teachings is another step boards can take. Finally, honestly measuring and addressing the culture, climate, and reality of your school and your board, through a diversity and equity audit, is a third step that boards can take toward ensuring they fully reflect and support the diversity needed to be the most effective, strategic governors.

Another type of diversity to consider is the diversity of thought. This is separate from the diversity of background/perspective. Diversity of thought refers to flexible thinking, being able to consider a topic or discussion from different angles, and not getting caught or stuck in one viewpoint. Diversity of thought can be taught, and each of us can practice thinking flexibly. A group may be quite culturally diverse and yet agree on everything (thereby not demonstrating diversity of thought) or a group might be very homogenous in outward appearance and yet be able to think flexibly and consider robust differences of opinion and view. As boards consider who they need, taking into account who is able to think flexibly or to learn how to think flexibly will be important. (See Chapter 3 for more on diversity of thought.)

With the understanding that your board needs to be as diverse as possible, one that reflects your community, represents a wide range of perspectives, and is able to think flexibly, you are now equipped to go through the process of identifying and recruiting new members.

VETTING POTENTIAL BOARD MEMBERS

Creating a process for considering candidates for board service, and regularly following this process completely, will help your governance committee reduce bias in their decision-making. This process includes how you will evaluate candidates through interviews and the material they share, how you will inform candidates about the board, and how your board will make decisions about inviting a candidate to join. A clearly articulated and regularly followed process supports objective discernment. In order to establish an unbiased process for vetting new board members, governance committee members will need to make decisions that will frame and shape each step of the process. These decisions include:

- What materials will be requested from potential candidates (for example: a resume, letter of intent, or list of prior volunteer experience)?

- Who will review candidate materials, and when will they review them (timelines and deadlines)?

- What questions will be asked during an interview with each candidate?

- What information will be shared with candidates (for example: the board member job description, handbook, and/or contract) to enable them to make an informed decision about joining your board?

- What specific criteria will be used to determine if a candidate will be brought to the board for consideration?

- When and how will candidates be presented to the board and how will decisions be made regarding confirming new board members?

Once governance committee members have answered these questions, they can articulate the vetting steps and obtain approval for the process from the full board.

ORIENTING NEW BOARD MEMBERS

Once you have identified your new board members, you will need to start the process of orienting them to your board. As you design your new board member orientation process, remember that typical adult learning doesn't always happen through a "one and done" encounter. We need reinforcement for learning new material, as well as the opportunity to apply new learning experientially. Here are some steps that can help this process.

1   Invite new board members to a board orientation where you
    go over the basic expectations and structure of your board.
    Provide them with board materials, including the bylaws, board
    handbook, job descriptions (for board members, board chair,
    and committee chairs), and potentially a board book such as
    this one to provide further resources. You will also provide them
    with the annual documents for them to sign, including the board
    contract and conflict of interest statement. If possible, the head
    of school and the board chair should be at this orientation; other
    board members may attend as well. At this orientation, include:

    - A tour of the school
    - A discussion of your bylaws
    - A discussion of your handbook
    - A discussion of job descriptions
    - An explanation of the board contract and
      conflict of interest statement
    - A time for questions

2 Facilitate another brief board orientation time during your board retreat, including all board members. All members benefit from going over key reminders regarding the handbook and bylaws. And all members will need to sign the conflict of interest statement.

3 Provide professional development for board members regarding governance. This can be an online program, an in-person workshop, or a set of readings. It can be conducted at a board retreat at the beginning of the year or in smaller chunks, at each board meeting throughout the year. This recognizes that the roles and responsibilities of independent school board members are typically new for most people. In each of these cases, follow-up from the professional development will be important to assimilate new understanding into the expectations and culture of your particular board.

4 Establish a mentor relationship for each new board member, someone they can talk with regarding any questions they have during the first year. Ask each mentor to be proactive about reaching out and connecting with the new board member.

5. Establish a time, after two or three meetings, for the board chair to meet with new board members to check in concerning their experience so far on the board. This is another opportunity for new members to ask questions and gain clarity, and indicates the recognition that they are still developing in their comfort level with the board.

Boards have a responsibility to ensure that they have the right people who have the right training serving on the board to accomplish the work of governing their school. This responsibility is critical, as the qualities, characteristics, skills, and abilities of the members of your school board determine how well it will be able to govern. And yet, too often, boards do not give this responsibility the attention or time it deserves. Establishing a series of processes to oversee the work of identifying needs, articulating who would add to the board, and then vetting and orienting new members will enable the board to build a robust, effective, and diverse membership.

BOARD CONTRACT AND CONFLICT OF INTEREST STATEMENT

Just as good fences make good neighbors, good contracts make good board members. A contract spells out the expectations between two parties. It provides board members the opportunity to affirm that they understand and agree to the stated expectations. A contract helps to prevent misunderstanding and confusion. Boards should develop a simple contract that they ask each board member to sign annually, outlining their expectations, such as attendance at meetings, preparation for meetings, participation in development and fundraising, confidentiality, and anything else important to upholding the school's culture and goals. A sample contract is offered in Appendix 3, but each board needs to customize their board member contract to reflect their own expectations.

Likewise, a conflict of interest statement, signed annually by each board member, provides clarity and transparency. Board conflicts of interest include any relationship in which a board member might have a financial or personal connection to the school: as a current parent, grandparent, employee, partner of an employee, a vendor, or other connected relationship. There will almost always be board members who have conflicts of interest on a board; this is not necessarily a problem. Indeed, it is helpful to have board members with close connections to the school. It is critical, however, to identify where conflict of interest may arise and to protect against situations where a board member may have difficulty fulfilling their duty of loyalty to put the needs and interests of the school first. By completing a conflict of interest statement annually, and sharing these with the whole board, board members can help one another stay true to their legal responsibility and duty to the school.

_____

QUESTIONS TO ASK YOUR BOARD

Do we have a Governance Committee in place that takes on the responsibilities of recruiting, orienting, and training a diverse group of board members?

Does our Governance Committee have a well-articulated process for recruiting and orienting new board members?

Do our board members reflect the diversity of our school and community?

Do we practice diversity of thought on our board?

Do our board members sign a board contract and a conflict of interest statement annually?

5

CULTURE, CLIMATE, EQUITY, INCLUSION & BELONGING

Inclusion is not a matter of political correctness. It is the key to growth.

REV. JESSE JACKSON

A s I write this, there is increasing conversation in the education world (and in many areas of the wider US population) regarding the need to more adequately address culture and climate, equity, inclusion, access, and belonging within our schools. These conversations are punctuated by the more focused lens on racial-justice issues in response to the continuing highly publicized attacks and murders of BIPOC (Black, Indigenous, People of Color) and other non-dominant groups. In many cases, these conversations within and about schools are heated, fueled by anger, fear, and frustrations. And yet these are not new conversations; the need for educators at all levels to address culture and climate, equity, inclusion, access, and belonging has always been there. Unfortunately, private and independent school boards have not succeeded in leading the way in addressing these issues.

Following the resurgence of the Black Lives Matter movement in response to the killings of Ahmaud Arbery, George Floyd, Breonna Taylor, and countless others during the first part of 2020, many schools across the country were forced by their constituents and their consciences to take a deep and honest look at how they were engaging with their BIPOC constituents. Both current and former students and families expressed their displeasure with schools because of past and current racism and discrimination in a variety of ways, including through social media posts such as those linked with the hashtag "#Black@." Many schools that had previously been complacent regarding anti-racism, equity, and inclusion were forced to address these issues. This work is often difficult, and it has proved challenging for many school communities. My colleagues who consult on issues of diversity, equity, inclusion, and belonging began to have more work than they could manage, supporting schools that needed to better understand and implement anti-racism, equity, and inclusion as a system.

In my opinion, this work is long overdue. It is challenging work for people of all social identifiers, and yet we must engage in this effort with purpose, diligence, and consistency—because equity and inclusion are at the heart of the culture and climate of an organization. And we know that culture and climate significantly impact an organization's ability to be successful. Social justice, culture, and climate are intertwined, each informing and influencing the others. If independent school boards are charged with ensuring the long-term viability and success of their schools, they must consider and address culture, climate, equity, and inclusion at all levels, starting with their own group. This is not extra work; it is essential and critical to everything that a board does.

Early in my career as a head search consultant, I took a job to help a small school find its next head of school. The former head of school had resigned in February but had agreed to stay on until the end of the school year. They had a trusted community member serving as an interim head of school for the next year while we searched for a more permanent one. I was aware that there were problems with leadership and governance, but did not know until after placing the new head of school the severity of the problem. At the beginning of the search process, as I conducted focus groups and interviews with board members, faculty and staff, parents, and community members, it became clear that there were factions or "sides" on the board. One side liked and supported the outgoing head of school and wanted her to stay; the other wanted her to leave. Nonetheless, as the head of school had resigned, I thought I would be able to work with the board to move forward with optimism in hiring and supporting a new leader. My meetings with them as individuals and as a group were productive, and we were able to find and hire a candidate who seemed to be a great match for their little school. I concluded that engagement with the feeling that I had served them well. However, several months into her appointment, the new head of school contacted me with great concern. The board was imploding. The chair had quit. The divide continued, but now the sides were being redrawn regarding funds and budgets and there was a lack of transparency, even with her, regarding the finances of the school. Individual board members began campaigning neutral board members to join sides. The new head of school left after serving for eight months because of the fractured board.

This school lost two heads in two years because of problems with board culture and climate. Lack of trust, honesty, transparency, and integrity all contributed to a breakdown in their ability to govern effectively. Each of those board members believed they were working in the best interest of the school, but because they were not able to work collaboratively and collegially, they ultimately harmed their school. Working with this school gave me firsthand experience of how critical board culture and climate are to the success of a school.

The now famous saying "culture eats strategy for breakfast," has been often discussed and promotes the belief in the business world that the human side of commerce is ignored at a business leader's peril. Organizations can focus all they want on goals and outcomes, can spend money and time on strategic plans, building upgrades, and market research, and yet they will never fully reach their potential if they have a destructive community environment. How people interact with one another, how included and valued they feel, and how meaningful the work is, each has a significant impact on the ability of an organization to be successful. I believe this to be true in all settings, and schools are no exception.

The terms *culture* and *climate* are often used interchangeably and yet they mean different things. *Culture* refers to the norms, traditions, and behaviors that members of an organization or group share. These patterns of behavior are often "invisible" or unexamined and usually are considered "the way we do things around here." The pattern of behavior, or culture of a group, is relatively stable, as changing behaviors takes time. *Climate* refers to the feelings and perceptions that community or group members hold relative to the group or organization. These feelings and perceptions can change more quickly than culture, as community members' feelings and perceptions can shift depending on various circumstances. Culture and climate inform and influence one another; a person's behaviors impact how they feel, and how they feel impacts how they act. Culture and climate are also at the intersection of an organization's ability to enable all their members to experience equity, inclusivity, and belonging. From a school leader's perspective, understanding the dynamics of culture and climate, and how each can be positively cultivated, is critical for both the health and the success of their organization.

As noted above, currently there is a lot of discussion in the US about "diversity, equity, inclusion, and belonging," often given the acronym DEIB, and usually lumped all together. However, these words also mean different things. To simplify, diversity is about representation—who is in attendance and how they self-identify.

Do your board members represent diverse racial and ethnic backgrounds, sexual orientation and identification, socioeconomic status, ages, and religions? Diversity does not address how the members feel once they are included. We can invite a variety of people to join our board and still not fully include or give them equal access to resources, time, authority, or influence, or fully welcome them to ensure that they feel they belong. I therefore use these words—*diversity, equity, inclusion,* and *belonging* (DEIB)—separately and talk about them in different ways, in different places. We need to consider diversity when we are thinking about *whom* to recruit to our small school boards. We need to address equity, inclusion, access, and belonging when we are considering the culture and climate of our boards and schools.

And we cannot talk about diversity, equity, inclusion, access, and belonging in the United States without acknowledging the dominant culture that has permeated our collective and individual mindsets, norms, perspectives, and behaviors. Racism, sexism, and classism have been upheld for centuries in our country, and it will take time and work to dismantle them. This is work that needs to be done by all people, in collaboration with one another. It is work that must be conducted through partnerships between those who enjoy privileges and those who have been disadvantaged. This is not work to be done *for* another person or group, but an opportunity for each of us to look into ourselves and understand the influence of culture and society on our own thoughts, perceptions, understandings, and behaviors.

I can think of no better place to do the work of dismantling our cultural inequities than in an independent school boardroom, although this may seem paradoxical, as private schools are inherently discriminatory. With our admissions processes structured to admit "mission-aligned students," we deny access to those who are not "mission-aligned." Nonetheless, our schools have an opportunity to examine our enrollment and hiring practices and expand our inclusion of people whom our missions *can* serve. Furthermore, we can work to promote and ensure equity for and inclusion of those in our communities. Especially in our small schools where we share a common characteristic of "close community," we can and should lead the way in promoting diversity (in all forms) that is supported by equity, inclusion, and belonging. Boards can and should serve as a model in this endeavor. There is a growing body of support to help this effort that highlights the work individuals need to do to understand dominant culture structures and their place within those structures, as well as how groups can engage in norm-setting that minimizes bias and maximizes welcoming behaviors. Furthermore, there is indication that the boards that spend time and attention on DEIB practices have a higher degree of organizational effectiveness (BoardSource 2021; Hayes 2017). Boards will be able to focus effectively on establishing the culture and climate that will best support their schools when they have spent the time examining their own relationships to privilege and power.

CULTURE

In order to address the behaviors, norms, traditions, and rituals that make up the culture of an organization, we must make visible much of what is invisible. One definition of *culture* is "shared patterns of behaviors and interactions, cognitive constructs and understanding that are learned by socialization" (Zimmerman 2017). Our behaviors are a result of our beliefs and values, and many people have never considered or challenged these fundamental aspects of their thought patterns. Beliefs and values develop from birth and reflect those of caregivers and others in our environments. We learn how to act and think through the socialization of our families and communities, and typically do not question these thoughts and beliefs or whether there are different options for thinking and behaving. When we encounter "other" cultures with different patterns of behaviors and thinking, we often don't merely label them as different, we label them as "wrong."

In order to understand how to fully engage effectively in a group made up of individuals from different backgrounds, experiences, and cultures, we need to examine our own behaviors, beliefs, and thought patterns and recognize judgments we make about "right and wrong." For example, if we believe that all students have the potential to learn and grow, we will behave in ways that support that belief. If instead, we believe that some students have limits on what they can learn, and how much they can grow, we will behave accordingly. In the boardroom, if we believe that each member has valuable insights to share, regardless of race, education, experience, gender, religion, or other social identifiers, we will respond differently than if we believe that some have more value than others. We need to communicate our understanding of these invisible patterns and intentionally create patterns that will be inclusive and supportive of all.

Our values are those sets of beliefs we hold regarding what is good, desirable, and worthwhile. Because values are worded positively, articulating shared values is a helpful way for a group to make fundamental beliefs visible. Boards can periodically engage in values clarification exercises to uncover beliefs, create a shared language, and agree upon productive behaviors. There are many examples of values clarification exercises that can be found in the literature and online. What is most important is to come to an agreement on the shared values that will guide and be a touchstone for your group and then to articulate the behaviors that demonstrate each value. Linking values to behaviors is critical, as it is the behaviors that are visible and can be addressed and changed to be in alignment with community values.

An example of a value might be respect. Respect is a value that is often cited as important and necessary by groups, and yet it may look very different to different people. This can be a problem when what one person thinks is respectful is seen as disrespectful by another. Try this: Think about a time when you showed respect to another person. What did that look like and sound like? Think about a time when someone showed respect to you. What did that look like and sound like? Think about a time when you witnessed someone being disrespectful. What did that look like and sound like? Now, imagine that other members of your board shared their examples of respect and disrespect. Do you think their examples would be similar to or different from yours? When a group can share these examples, you can begin to craft a picture of what respect looks like to your whole group. And you can follow this exercise by agreeing upon a set of behaviors that will demonstrate respect to all members of the group. The result is that you will have a shared understanding and language around respect that was previously invisible or unspoken.

Agreeing on sets of behaviors that demonstrate your shared values is the first step toward addressing the norms of your board. Norms are behaviors that are accepted, expected, encouraged, or discouraged in a group. Expected norms on some school boards might be that everyone attends board meetings unless they are truly unable, and that board members show up for meetings on time. Other school boards may accept that board members show up late, and those behaviors are not addressed or corrected. Some boards may have behavioral norms that discourage people from asking a lot of questions during meetings or posing questions that diverge from the majority held opinion. The behavioral norms of a group may be invisible to some; they may not recognize the patterns the group has developed. Making these behavioral patterns visible and considering if they are beneficial will enable your board to be more effective in its work.

Over time, groups also develop traditions and tangible evidence that support and demonstrate their values and beliefs. These are external representations of what the school and board believe to be important and valuable. An example of a tradition might be the annual school fundraising golf tournament held by the board that board members are expected to support financially and with their participation. Golf is an expensive and exclusive sport. Not all members of a truly diverse board may be interested in or able to help fund a golf tournament. If this is a long-held tradition for the school, there may be conflict over the values and beliefs that the tournament represents. Boards will need to carefully consider traditions, as well as other tangible evidence (posters at the school, website pictures, brochures, and other visual displays) that represent the values and beliefs that they want to convey.

CLIMATE

Think about the exercise above to consider the value of respect and then imagine sharing with the members of your board (or another group) your own examples of what respect and disrespect look like to you. How do you feel about sharing these examples? Do you expect that your examples will be valued, or do you fear they may be dismissed or subtly shamed? You are now thinking about your own sense of emotional safety in the group. Would you feel comfortable sharing those examples with those group members? If you would feel comfortable, you likely have some sense of emotional safety, that your sense of self will be honored and respected. If you would not feel comfortable sharing in your group, perhaps there is not a sense of emotional safety for you—you fear feeling shamed, discounted, or not validated. These feelings are a part of the climate of the group. This illustrates why, if the climate of the group is not positive and safe for all, it is difficult to focus on culture and changing behaviors before focusing on feelings and perceptions.

Climate refers to a more transient set of perceptions about a group than culture. People develop opinions and perceptions about group dynamics based on their experiences over time and how they make meaning of those experiences. Do they believe that group members are supportive and inclusive, or do they feel that they are distant, judgmental, and unwelcoming? These feelings will have a tremendous impact on how each member of the group interacts with others, is able to participate in conversations and decision-making, and contributes to the goals and efforts of the group. There are five main elements that contribute to group climate:

- *Agency* The feeling of control individuals have over the work and their place in the group
- *The nature of relationships* Includes trust, respect, honesty, inclusion
- *Meaningful work* The value placed on the work or effort
- *Achievement and recognition* Individuals understanding what it takes to achieve, and feel recognized for achievements
- *Accountability* A sense that all are held equitably accountable

CHANGING CULTURE AND CLIMATE

Where does a board start when they want to impact or change their culture or climate? How does the board know what issues need to be addressed? Here are two sets of questions you can ask to begin deciding a course of action:

1 How do people feel about this group? Are relationships positive? Is there a sense of agency, achievement, and accountability? How do we know about their feelings (are we guessing, have people said things directly, are we witnessing behaviors that indicate certain feelings)? Do we need to gather more information about how people feel (through a survey or interviews)?

2 What behaviors does this group have that help create and maintain a positive culture? This might include how engaged members

are, how and when they communicate, who communicates, who stays silent, and where power and authority are held. What actions by board members as individuals or a group might be contributing to a less-than-positive culture?

These initial questions can help guide you to your next steps. If the climate needs to be addressed, if you have the sense that there are feelings or perceptions within the group that are negative (particularly around emotional safety, inclusion, and/or belonging), then you will need to address this first. If there is a general sense of positivity within the group regarding feelings and perceptions, you can look at bolstering your culture.

To address culture, and work toward changing behaviors, here are five areas to address:

1 Make sure your values and connected behavioral norms, aligned with your school's mission, are clearly and consistently stated.
2 Make sure your written and stated expectations, policies, and procedures are clear and complete and reflect your shared values.
3 Hold all people accountable to your stated expectations, policies, and procedures.
4 Measure climate: how people perceive the community environment.
5 Make your work on upholding a positive, inclusive, and equitable culture and climate visible by talking about it, reporting progress, and testing it regularly.

Actively and regularly addressing the culture and climate of a board and a school is a fundamental responsibility of board members and the head of school. Through this work, you support the ability for your board to be equitable and inclusive for all members, as well as to be able to engage in your work of governing effectively. And yet, with the emergencies and urgencies that small school boards so often face, culture and climate can get pushed down the priority list. I believe this is shortsighted. Healthy, positive board culture and climate are the foundation on which boards can address the needs of the school; they are prerequisites. Without healthy, positive, and productive culture and climate, the board will not have the ability to fully and effectively govern.

EQUITY, INCLUSION, AND BELONGING

Thankfully the body of knowledge is growing regarding how groups can work to ensure equity, inclusion, and belonging. Yet given the centuries of systemic racism, patriarchy, classism, homophobia, and other systems of exclusion in the US and globally, many, if not most, groups continue to need to intentionally and actively focus on how to be fully inclusive. The process of considering culture and climate assists in addressing equity, inclusion, and belonging; however, without a focus on specific potentially marginalized constituents, there is the possibility of overlooking their exclusion. For example, a school board may work diligently to increase their understanding of LGBTQ+ issues, to change their language, and ensure their processes and meetings are welcoming to members of different sexual orientations and gender identities. And yet they may not have done that work to include members from different ethnic and cultural backgrounds (such as those from Asian, African, or Hispanic descent). So this board is inclusive of some but not all of its members.

The work of creating a diverse, inclusive, equitable, and welcoming culture and climate for all school constituents must be ongoing for boards. This means intentionally and regularly ensuring that the values of the school and board are known, upheld, and "lived" in all aspects of the school's functioning. It also means intentionally and regularly working to understand how racism, discrimination, and exclusion continue to function in our society and taking steps to combat these forces within the board. This work needs to be disciplined and consistent, and boards can and should include professional development in this area annually. Boards must engage in this work both because it is the right thing to do and because creating a diverse, positive, inclusive, and equitable environment leads to organizational success.

QUESTIONS TO ASK YOUR BOARD

How do people feel about this group? Are relationships positive? Is there a sense of agency, achievement, accountability?

How do we know about their feelings (are we guessing, have people said things directly, are we witnessing behaviors that indicate certain feelings)? Do we need to gather more information about how people feel (through a survey or interviews)?

What behaviors does this group have that help create and maintain a positive culture? This might include how engaged members are, how and when they communicate, who communicates, etc.

What actions by board members as individuals or a group might be contributing to a less-than-positive culture?

Do we have a clearly articulated set of values that guide the work and interactions of the board? Have we articulated the behaviors that demonstrate these values?

PART THREE

———

THE RIGHT PRACTICES

6

———

GOAL SETTING
& PLANNING

———

*If you don't know exactly where you are going,
how will you know when you get there?*

STEVE MARABOLI, *LIFE, THE TRUTH, AND BEING FREE*

E ven though I arrived early every day, when I walked into my
school building as head of school, I was inundated with questions, problems to be solved, checks to sign, people to call.
When I finally made it to my desk and sat down, there were usually
one hundred new emails in my inbox, stacks of papers to address, and
meetings to plan. Often, it felt like chaos. In the beginning, I was perilously close to dropping one (or more) of the many balls I was juggling.
I've always been a fairly organized person, but my limits were tested
on a daily basis. I was forced to consider how I was managing my time,
energy, and focus in order to accomplish everything that was required
of me. I tried a variety of systems—calendars, lists, sticky notes—until I
found the ones that worked best for me. The most important thing
I learned was that I needed to regularly set aside protected time to

intentionally plan my work and priorities. With all the demands on my attention and the actions that were required of me, spending time and effort on the act of thinking through what I wanted to accomplish and creating an intentional plan for accomplishing my goals was key.

Small school board members frequently find themselves feeling as I did in those early years: overwhelmed. There is so much that is involved in effective governance and, typically, so many urgent problems to address. Therefore, small school boards in particular need to create time to intentionally and strategically set goals. In our close-knit communities, where we delight in interpersonal connections, there is a tendency for board meetings to be consumed by conversations about the life of the school. We love hearing about the projects students are working on, the successes of our faculty and staff, and the creative initiatives our administrators are implementing. These are important pieces of information, and yet engaging in long conversations about these topics does not accomplish the work of the board. Without specific, articulated goals, it is easy to go off topic and get "stuck in the weeds." Rather, boards need the discipline of identifying what they intend to accomplish and then holding themselves accountable for accomplishing their goals.

We all set goals for ourselves—sometimes formally, sometimes informally. When we think, *I'm going to finish that report this afternoon* or *I need to remember to call Mrs. Lee* we are setting goals. Given the nature of the work that needs to be accomplished to run and govern a school, there are a lot of goals that need to be set and met. Some of us are better than others at organizing our time, work, and energy to accomplish these goals. And there are a variety of strategies and systems one can find to support personal and group goal setting. From a board's perspective, their work needs to be guided by a series or hierarchy of goals, each developed through a planned, collaborative process, each focused on specific outcomes desired at different times and levels of their work. This hierarchy includes long-range goals, annual board goals, annual committee goals, annual head of school goals, and board and committee meeting goals. Let's consider each of these.

LONG-RANGE GOALS

When you go on a road trip, most often you have an end destination in mind. You don't just drive out of your driveway and start off down the road, randomly turning whenever the urge strikes. Rather, you identify where you are going and you head in that direction. In the days of yore, you probably looked at a map to plan out your route. Now we have GPS. Nonetheless, there are decisions to be made about the route you will take. Operating a school without identifying long-range goals is like driving around without a destination in mind.

A school's long-range goals are typically established through a strategic planning process. This process often includes articulating an organization's values, vision, priorities, and desired outcomes. I have found that when you mention strategic planning to folks, you can expect to get some eye rolls. The strategic planning of the past—time-consuming and laborious, resulting in the "binder-on-the-shelf" that is never touched again—has given this process a bad reputation. And yet I believe there is significant value in engaging in a regular community-wide effort to articulate a school's values, vision, priorities, and goals. Strategic planning can be conducted in a way that is engaging and meaningful and that produces a set of goals that actively support a school's work. When conducted well, a strategic planning process, and the resulting strategic plan itself, can unite a school board and administration around a shared understanding of its vision and identify the steps for achieving what the school is expecting to accomplish in the upcoming years.

Most independent school accrediting bodies require that schools engage in regular strategic planning. Yet they don't typically prescribe *how* to do this. Schools develop strategic plans at different times in their organizational lives and therefore need different types of plans. Some plans address specific problems or deficiencies that need to be corrected; some help schools to transform into better versions of themselves; and some are in response to crises. There are various ways to go about conducting a strategic plan, and schools can choose to hire consultants to lead them through the process or to facilitate it with internal community members. There is no requirement regarding how long this should take, how many goals should be developed, in what format the goals should be presented, or what the goals should target. Each of these considerations needs to be determined by the school, based on its current circumstances. Some schools want and benefit from a yearlong process that results in a multi-page document that establishes goals for the next five years or longer. Other schools want and benefit from a much shorter process that results in a one-page document that articulates a few targeted goals over a shorter period of time. Schools should not fall into the trap of thinking there is one size that fits all in strategic planning or that they need to conduct their next strategic plan the same way they did their last one.

The elements of a strategic plan can be crafted to make it a more iterative and responsive document. In the past, strategic plans ended up gathering dust on the shelf because they were static; the goals and action steps were developed at the beginning and were not reconsidered again as the plan was implemented over the years. We all know that "life happens"—we have enrollment surges and dips; we find new donors; there is a global recession or a global pandemic—each of these life occurrences provides challenges and opportunities that may change the way a school community thinks about its future and its goals. Or they may change the way the school approaches their goals. I therefore recommend that at the end of the data-gathering and goal/strategy-developing part of the strategic planning process, schools publish just their goals and strategies. The community needs to know where a school is headed and what its priorities are.

However, the action plan and annual implementation plan are internal documents that are developed to guide the work of accomplishing the plan. *How* the goals are met can be flexible and responsive to current circumstances.

Even if your school is not in a position to conduct a full, community-wide process to develop a strategic plan, all schools need some set of overarching goals to guide their work and to establish a foundation for other shorter-term goals. Small schools may find themselves in a position where they do not have the financial or human resources to conduct a full strategic plan. In this case, the head and board chair should draft a set of shorter-term, placeholder goals to guide their work until a more comprehensive strategic plan can be developed.

Here are some things to remember when strategic planning:

1 It is beneficial to clearly articulate the *outcomes* you want to achieve. What will your school look like, feel like, produce, experience, and celebrate when the plan has been implemented?

2 Your plan needs to be ambitious as well as achievable. Articulating the mundane may allow you to feel like you are accomplishing something, but does not propel your school forward. One the other hand, striving for the nearly impossible is, well, nearly impossible! Outlining goals that meaningfully move your school forward is what you need.

3 Strategic plans should not be a set of "other" goals that are disconnected from the everyday life of your school. They should be the foundation from which all other goals are created.

4 Including as many constituents as possible in thinking about and developing your strategic plan will promote not only buy-in, but also diversity of thought and perspective.

5 Establishing clear tools for measuring the success of your
   work, and sharing the results will provide accountability.

6 Continuing to meaningfully include constituents
   in the achievement of the plan goals maintains
   buy-in and diversity of thought.

7 Creating a mechanism for reviewing action steps to
   achieve goals on a regular basis will allow your plan to be
   responsive to current conditions and circumstances.

Setting goals for the school, the head, and for itself is a foundational activity for any board. Goals provide a roadmap for focus, work,
and energy, establish a common language, and result in a method for
holding the board accountable. Too many boards fall into the trap of
thinking they do not have enough time to spend on careful, strategic goal setting, when in fact, crafting clear, focused goals will enable
them to use their time more efficiently and productively. A long-range
(or strategic) plan is important in conveying to a community the
direction and priorities of the organization. This plan is critical for
the head and the board because it provides the map for planning out
all the other work of running and stewarding the school. Then, these
long-range goals provide the foundation for setting annual goals.

ANNUAL GOAL SETTING

A board chair once contacted me and asked to talk about board
evaluation. His board had not previously conducted an evaluation
and thought it would be helpful. I agreed; board evaluation is a
critical tool in helping boards identify how to be most effective (see
Chapter 13). He began by asking me what the evaluation should
measure. When I responded by asking him what his board's annual

goals were, he stammered—they hadn't identified any goals, they just met monthly and discussed the topics that seemed most relevant in the moment.

I confront this frequently—boards that conduct their business without any specific direction, expectation, or desired outcomes; they just do their work and hope it is effective. Setting annual goals is one of the first things a board should do every year. Time should be set aside by the board leadership to begin the planning discussions, and the full board should participate in articulating goals for itself. This planning does not need to be onerous or time consuming. It does need to be intentional, purposeful, and well-communicated. The most common structure for goal setting, and the one that is the easiest in my opinion to implement, is the SMART framework. When creating goals, make sure they are:

S Specific

M Measurable

A Achievable

R Relevant

T Time-bound

There are three types of goals boards should set for themselves:

1 Regular goals that fulfill basic board responsibilities
2 Periodic goals
3 Annual goals

Regular goals are those that address annual tasks such as setting tuitions, approving a budget, approving new board members, considering a strategic financial plan, and evaluating the head and the board itself. These are the types of things boards often do on autopilot without establishing specific goals to guide their accomplishments. Yet by taking the time to consider how these tasks will be accomplished and what boards hope to achieve regarding each, better outcomes can be realized. Periodic goals include strategic planning, accreditation, and updating bylaws, activities that don't occur every year and that can be planned for over time. Setting a multiyear calendar that indicates when your board plans to engage in these big, periodic activities will help you spread them out so they will not all occur at once.

Annual goals are accomplishments that boards hope to achieve over the coming year. They should be linked to the overall school goals, as articulated by the strategic plan. The number of annual board goals should be limited each year in order to be able to fully focus and ensure you achieve them (please don't make a laundry list of accomplishments to achieve!). Some examples of annual goal topics include the following:

- Board efficacy, including improving board meetings, establishing a more strategic and inclusive recruitment process, examining and enhancing DEI/culture on the board, and other effective governance practices
- Considering the mission-program-message-market alignment of the school and where it might be improved (see Chapter 10)
- Enhancing financial forecasting processes and procedures; enhancing dashboard reporting (see Chapter 11)
- Developing a more robust head support process (see Chapter 9)
- Developing a more robust crisis plan (see Chapter 14)

Boards that spend time crafting sets of shared goals for themselves for the year, at least some of which support the achievement of the school's strategic plan goals, will be able to focus their work and efforts and will accomplish more in committees and at each board meeting. They will also be able to measure their efficacy at the end of the year against these goals. Likewise, committees should develop annual goals for themselves that will enable them to support and promote their board's annual goals. Boards and committees without annual goals typically find that they have less clarity about topic and focus when they are creating their agendas and they are less able to measure their efficacy.

Once you have established overall strategic goals for the school and annual goals for the board and committees, it is much easier to identify what each meeting will need to accomplish. When I was a head of school, our board created an annual calendar for our meetings. There were certain months where we knew in advance what topics we needed to address and we filled our calendar with these regular goals first: the full-day board retreat in September; strategic financial plan in October; tuition-setting in December; diversity, equity, and inclusion consideration in January; school visit in February; admissions in March; new member presentation in April; and the annual meeting in June. We wove our specific annual goals around these regular topics. The key was to articulate these goals at the beginning of the year to the entire board so that committee members could plan how they would structure their meetings to support the work of the full board.

The next chapter on facilitating effective meetings dives deeper into how to accomplish meeting goals. The key is to plan well in advance and to be clear about the specific outcomes that are desired for each meeting. Then, crafting detailed, clear agendas helps all members to understand expectations and keeps the meeting focused on outcomes.

HEAD OF SCHOOL GOALS

The hierarchy of goal setting that started with strategic planning comes to its conclusion with the setting of annual goals for the head of school. Articulating clear expectations for major accomplishments will bring the head of school and the board onto the same page and will provide clarity and accountability. Given the head of school's unique position of knowing far more about the nuances and needs of the school than any board member ever could, having a board develop goals for a head of school without any collaboration is fruitless. This process should be undertaken together, taking into account the needs of the school, the board, and the head school themself.

Creating annual head of school goals can be tricky for some schools. They question how many goals there should be, what level of specificity and focus to develop, and how best to follow up with evaluation and accountability. I think of head of school goals in four categories:

1. Goals that support the accomplishment of the responsibilities set out in their contract and job description. This is the primary work of the head. Some boards and heads assume that as these are basic goals to be accomplished, they do not need to be specifically articulated in a set of annual head's goals. Other schools reference the achievement of these basic responsibilities as the first of the head's annual goals.

2. Goals that support the accomplishment of the school's goals. For example, goals such as facilitating accreditation self-study work groups or facilitating the process to create a new marketing plan.

3. Goals that correct personal leadership weaknesses. These could include improving group facilitation skills or improving a staff evaluation process.

4. Goals that support personal/professional growth. These are primarily driven by the head's desires and can be in any realm.

Similar to the board's annual goals, the head of school's annual goals should be written as SMART goals, should include no more than three to five meaningful, relevant, and attainable goals, and the board and head of school should develop a plan for discussing the achievement of these goals throughout the year. At the end of the year, accountability to the achievement of the head of school's annual goals can be one part of the process of overall evaluation of their performance. We go more into this evaluation in Chapter 9.

THE WHY OF GOAL SETTING

The psychology of goal setting tells us that intentionally setting goals for ourselves that are clear, attainable, and meaningful helps us to be more productive and even satisfied when the goals are accomplished (Chowdhury 2021; Riopel 2021). Clearly articulated goals provide a focus for discussion and effort and help groups to develop and understand a shared vision. Establishing goals provides clarity for everyone involved; the head of school and board members are clear about what is expected of themselves and of others. And clear goals allow for clear accountability. Conversely, without clear goals, evaluating individual and/or group efficacy is challenging and can devolve into opinions that are colored by bias.

I also like to use Simon Sinek's "Getting to Why" perspective when considering goal setting. He articulated the difference organizations can make when they focus on *why* they are in business and then distinguish this from *what* they are doing and *how* they are doing it. In goal setting, I think we benefit from starting by first understanding why we have set our goals and then focusing on how we will achieve them. We often create goals that appear to be meaningful without spending the time to think about whether they are the right goals. By spending time and attention on thoughtfully establishing goals, we provide the foundation for effective strategic thinking.

When developing annual goals for the board as a whole and for each committee, remember the following:

1 SMART goals (specific, measurable, attainable, relevant, and time-bound) are most helpful.

2 Too many goals will be unattainable and overwhelming. Aim for no more than three to five goals for the board and for each committee. Of course, boards and committees will achieve many things over the course of a year. The three to five stated goals will serve as a framework and guide for determining all of the other actions and sub-goals for each body.

3 Create a process and timeline for considering achievement of your goals throughout the year. Adjust as necessary.

QUESTIONS TO ASK YOUR BOARD

Do we have a set of goals to guide the accomplishment of our school's mission and vision, and annual full board and committee work?

Do we spend sufficient time creating meaningful, relevant goals?

How are we measuring progress toward the achievement of our goals?

7

FACILITATING
EFFECTIVE MEETINGS

As a leader, you must consistently drive effective communication.
Meetings must be deliberate and intentional—your organizational
rhythm should value purpose over habit and effectiveness over efficiency.

CHRIS FUSSELL, "THE BIGGEST CAREER LESSON
THIS NAVY SEAL LEARNED IN IRAQ"

I had recently joined the board and was eager to be supportive, yet I was dreading the next committee meeting. I was trying not to step on anyone's toes—I was the new person and needed to understand the culture and climate that had been established—but I didn't think I would be able to sit through many more of these meetings. The full-board meetings were run relatively well (although there was room for improvement). However, the meeting I had attended of the committee on which I was serving was painful. There was no agenda. We showed up (on Zoom, because this was during the COVID-19 pandemic) and the chair of the committee posed a question at the beginning and committee members began talking. The conversation meandered onto various topics and I wasn't at all sure what our goal was. Two committee members, who clearly had a history of disagreeing with one another, got into an argument (over what seemed to me to be a trivial issue). I tried to ask questions that would help focus our conversation onto a specific issue that would result in a decision or action, but the discussion kept veering off onto random topics. At the end of the two-hour meeting, I wasn't sure what had been accomplished. And later I realized that no notes had been taken.

The unfortunate fact is that many people who lead or facilitate meetings are doing it poorly. When meetings are unfocused, boring, confusing, ineffective, and/or a waste of time, it makes participants feel frustrated, disrespected, disconnected, and even angry. Poorly led meetings can happen either in-person or virtually, as we have found out in 2020–2022 during the pandemic when all our meetings were conducted online. Virtual meetings add a layer of complication as participants can turn off their video and audio and truly disconnect, whereas in-person meetings have a social code that says one must at least appear to be paying attention (although the surreptitious looking at cell phones certainly happens). When I think about all the time and talent that are underused or wasted because of carelessly planned and facilitated meetings, it astonishes me. Facilitating productive, engaging, and meaningful meetings is not impossible, although it takes some effort, planning, and forethought. For boards—whose members' time is so very precious, and whose charge is so important—it is imperative that meetings are as effective as they possibly can be.

Group meetings are important for a variety of reasons, such as developing shared understandings, considering new ideas, developing strategies to meet goals, crafting solutions to problems, learning new content, and building community and culture. Yet when organizational leaders plan regular meetings (staff meetings, board meetings, committee meetings, etc.) we tend to go on autopilot, focusing only on the content of the meeting without considering the process. We often don't devote the time necessary to consider and plan for the context and structure that will fully engage group members and enable our meeting to be truly productive. This results in boring, unproductive meetings that not only waste people's time, but can harm a group's productivity, engagement, effort, and culture. It is not that group leaders are intentionally setting out to facilitate boring meetings—I know for myself there have been many times in the past when I realized upon reflection that I fell short in engaging my meeting participants in a productive gathering. As I considered the glazed eyes, slow responses to my questions, and quick departures at the end, I knew I could have done more to be a better facilitator. But I didn't have a guide, a roadmap for how to lead productive and effective meetings.

We know a lot about how people learn; what helps improve the application of learning as well as what factors hinder learning. We know about group dynamics and how people can engage effectively with one another. We know about motivation: what conditions and circumstances increase motivation, and what can be demotivating. We know about decision-making and the factors that improve decision-making outcomes. And yet leaders who plan regular meetings rarely apply these sets of knowledge when they invite participants to their weekly or monthly gatherings. Often agendas are loosely put together and are carbon copies of previous agendas (see the discussion at the beginning of Chapter 3). There are few if any prompts to prepare participants for the meeting and if there is required reading (such as reports) they are not sent far enough in advance so that participants can fully digest them. There is often little attention paid to how the group engages with the material during the meeting. Rather, topics are considered in the big group and those folks who are quick processors and are comfortable, confident group speakers dominate the conversation. And there is rarely significant attention paid to how the group interacts, and the behaviors and feelings that impact group dynamics, such as culture, climate, equity, inclusion, and belonging. The end result can be that some participants are left out, discussions devolve into off-topic ramblings or arguments, too much time is spent on some topics and not enough on others, and meetings conclude without deciding or accomplishing much of anything.

Yet, with a bit of time and thought, regular meetings can be planned that will be more engaging for participants, result in achieving desired, articulated outcomes, and, ultimately, that will create a team that is cohesive and productive.

In Priya Parker's beautifully written book, *The Art of Gathering: How We Meet and Why It Matters* (ParkerPenguin Business 2018), she describes in detail the different phases of planning for meetings and how to consider the participants' experience at each step of the way. She begins: "The way we gather matters. Gatherings consume our days and help determine the kind of world we live in, in both our intimate and public realms. Gathering—the conscious bringing together of people for a reason—shapes the way we think, feel, and make sense of the worldAnd yet most of us spend very little time thinking about the actual ways in which we gather."

In my work with small school leaders, I have found Ms. Parker's last statement. . . . to be true. In an attempt to maintain our close-knit collegiality in small schools, we sometimes try to avoid what feels like formality. We equate structure and procedures with rigidity or lack of connection. However, we risk effectiveness by not paying attention to good practices in meeting facilitation. If heads of schools and board chairs want to ensure that they are effectively using the skills and abilities of their board members, then they need to facilitate better, more effective meetings. They need to take themselves off autopilot and consider why they are facilitating a meeting, what their goals are, and how best to manage and use the strengths of the meeting participants to achieve their goals. Based on Parker's thinking, and incorporating learning from education, psychology, and sociology, here are five steps to planning and facilitating an effective meeting.

STEP 1: ARTICULATE YOUR PURPOSE

When I first became head of school, I held monthly staff meetings and attended the four board meetings that were scheduled each year. This is how the previous head of school had structured meetings, and rather than come up with something new, I followed her process. Shortly before each staff meeting, I met with the educational director and we decided what we would discuss. In my first year, our hour-and-a-half meetings were primarily information-sharing venues, with all thirty-three faculty and staff members sitting around in a big circle, mostly listening. As I think back, I cringe at how boring that must have been for them. No one ever complained, but I sensed a lack of energy and engagement after our meetings. Certainly no one looked forward to staff meetings. Our board meetings weren't much better. Board members read my head's report and asked me questions and then discussed the finance report. Our agendas looked the same each time we met, and we didn't accomplish much; we spent our time discussing and considering topics rather than making any decisions. Our primary problem with these meetings was we hadn't defined *why* we were meeting. We were on autopilot: meeting because that is what we had always done, not because we had a specific goal or purpose. Once we changed the way we thought about why we were bringing these groups of people together, our meetings became much more energized. More people participated, our conversations were focused, and there was a sense we had accomplished something meaningful at the end of each meeting. I actually once had a faculty member tell me she was eager to attend the upcoming staff meeting.

The first step in meeting planning is to ask yourself why you are bringing this particular group of people together at this particular time.

Even if this is a regularly scheduled board meeting, and you have established an annual board calendar with big topics identified for each meeting (see Chapter 6 for goal setting), spending the time to consider your specific meeting goals is important and will go a long way toward ensuring productive, engaged participants. What do you expect and want to happen, to achieve, and to feel at the end of this meeting? What will board members take away from this meeting? If you, as the facilitator, aren't clear about the purpose, no one will be. It may help to articulate (in writing, perhaps) exactly what the outcomes of the meeting will be; for example: *We will have a shared understanding of our values and a list of ways we demonstrate those values.* Or: *We will agree (vote) on the calendar for next year.*

When determining the purpose of a meeting, push yourself to go further than merely "to inform the board." Much of the information sharing that typically happens in a board meeting can occur in different ways such as email, reports, or short videos. Your time with the full board together as one is precious. You need to use it as wisely as possible to engage in discussion, decision-making, envisioning outcomes, planning, and team building that can't be done otherwise.

Agenda

Once you have articulated your goals and motivations, you can begin to create the meeting agenda. Agendas can serve several purposes:

- To inform participants of the topics to be covered
- To inform participants of what actions will be taken
- To inform participants what will be expected of them during the meeting
- To provide the facilitators with a structure they can use to remind participants of the objectives and redirect them when they go astray

FIGURE 7.1 **SAMPLE BOARD AGENDA**

XYZ SCHOOL BOARD OF TRUSTEES
April 20, 2019
6:00 P.M.

PROPOSED AGENDA

☐ Review and approve March minutes

☐ Reports:
    ☐ Head of School's Report
    ☐ Governance Committee Report
    ☐ Finance Report

☐ Old Business

☐ New Business

☐ Adjourn

- To serve as a basis for documenting what occurred at the meeting, what actions were taken, and what decisions were made

Agendas therefore need to be carefully and thoughtfully crafted. Unfortunately, I have seen (and, in all honesty, facilitated) many board meeting agendas that looked something like the sample in Figure 7.1.

As you can see, we did not articulate any specific goals for the meeting, and there was no indication that board members would be engaged in any strategic or visionary thinking during this meeting. It looks like another boring meeting. What I found from both attending and facilitating meetings that were guided by agendas such as this one is that sometimes there were great discussions. Sometimes we were able to think strategically about how to solve a problem or determine what path forward we should take. Sometimes we ended up with a specific action plan and assignments for individuals. And yet many other times I realized we had devolved into "admiring problems": talking in circles without crafting a way forward. Often we concluded our meeting and nothing had been decided, nothing had been accomplished. The problem with this type of agenda is that it is too nebulous and does not guide or focus discussion and decision-making.

There are several elements to a well-crafted agenda as illustrated in Figure 7.2:

FIGURE 7.2 **SAMPLE STRATEGIC BOARD AGENDA**

DATE		
PUBLIC		
TIME	TOPIC	DISCUSSION
11:00–11:05 A.M.	Welcome; approve agenda	
11:05–11:10	Consent agenda: 1) Approve last meeting minutes 2) Next meeting change to Sunday the 12th from 3–5 P.M.	
11:10–11:30	Consider Finance Committee dashboard; assumption testing	What assumptions are we making with this current model? Are they accurate and reasonable? What other assumptions might we test?
11:30 AM–12:00 PM	Small group thinking; future financial models	What are the potential threats to the current financial model in 2 years, 5 years, 10 years? What opportunities might we have to strengthen this model in the same time frame?
12–12:15	Consider Governance Committee, Head Support Committee, and Advancement Committee reports	Questions, comments, concerns?
12:15–12:30	Consider Head report	How might board members provide direct support?
12:50–1:00	Assign action items; plan for next meeting	

1 It is time-bound. Determine and articulate how much time you plan to spend on each topic. You can certainly alter this during the meeting, but having the time stamp on your agenda keeps you focused on the efficient use of time.

2 It is topic-focused. Unlike the general agenda above that only identified the reports to be considered, effective agendas specify what the conversation will target.

OUTCOME/DECISION	SUPPORTING DOCUMENTS	FOLLOW-UP ACTION NEEDED
	October minutes	
Approval of Finance Committee dashboard	Draft dashboard report	
List ways members can provide direct support		

What specific topic will you discuss or decide? There are times when open discussion or questioning a report is necessary. State this. Rather than just listing "Head's Report," you might list "Questions regarding Head's Report" and give this five to ten minutes. Or you might list a topic covered in the Head's Report, such as "How will we best use the gym during weekends?—(as referenced in the Head's Report)."

3   It articulates goals. State what you expect to accomplish. You may want to make a decision, generate a list of possibilities, or develop shared language or understanding. Be clear on the agenda what your goals and outcomes are for each topic.

4   It provides the opportunity to identify follow-up actions and expectations. A well-crafted agenda leads to action. The action may be in the form of a specific behavior (John will inform the admin team . . .), a committee task (the Governance Committee will discuss what training is needed . . .), or a thought exercise (board members will consider what factors impact . . .). This section may also address how information that was discussed and decided upon will be shared outside the board.

Meeting facilitators who are most successful go beyond merely setting the agenda and goals in this first step of identifying the purpose of their meeting and also consider the environmental context of the meeting. In order to be most successful, where should this meeting be held? What meeting space will best support the outcomes we want to achieve? When should it be held to ensure the best outcomes? How long should this meeting be? Should there be food and drinks? It is easy to overlook these questions, especially when your meeting is a recurring one. And it is possible that the answer to these questions is that your meeting should be the same as it was last time. Nonetheless, meeting facilitators who consider these environmental context questions each time they plan a meeting will craft a more intentional and responsive meeting.

STEP 2: PREPARE MEETING PARTICIPANTS

Once you have established why you are meeting, what you hope to accomplish, and what external factors will help your meeting be successful, consider how you can motivate participants to be ready to engage. Sometimes, although not always, it is beneficial to have meeting participants actively prepare for the meeting beforehand. They might read a report or article, watch a video, respond to a brief survey, or merely ponder a question or two. Thinking about your participants' experience before the meeting sets them up to be well-informed and prepared. What materials do they need? Are there prompts, activities, or readings you could provide before the meeting that would "prime the pump" for participants? Parker tells us in *The Art of Gathering* that "90 percent of what makes a gathering successful is put in place beforehand" (Parker 2018). Yet for board meeting facilitators, this step is sometimes easier said than done. With the incredibly busy schedules heads of schools and board chairs have, creating time to think through and plan how to engage board members can be difficult. Therefore, some of this task can be delegated to committees. As discussed in Chapter 8, committees do the prework of the board, helping to frame the questions and prompts that support board discussions and decisions. Committee chairs can support the board chair and head of school in preparing board members to be active participants in meetings. With your purpose and stated meeting outcomes in mind, what materials do your board members need in order to be prepared for the conversations that will lead to decisions and actions? How much time do they need to read and consider the materials? Take into account your board members' busy lives and personal preferences; you will need to give them ample lead time before the scheduled meeting.

Next, think about *how* you want the board to use the information they have been given. Is there a decision to be made? Is there more information needed? Can the information be interpreted in different ways? How can the information be applied? These are the types of questions you can ask board members to consider *before* the meeting so they can be fully prepared to make decisions, offer suggestions, and provide different perspectives during the meeting. You could also provide them with a scenario and ask them to consider how they might handle it; or send a short survey that you can tally and use results during the meeting. Your pre-meeting prompts and questions will need to be developed in response to your stated meeting objectives.

STEP 3: SET THE STAGE FOR A SUCCESSFUL MEETING

I am a very outcome-oriented person, and often when leading meetings have had a tendency to start quickly, right on time, jumping directly into agenda items. However, this abrupt start overlooks an important opportunity to fully engage and welcome meeting participants. Consider creating a bridge from the outside world into the world of your meeting. When facilitators spend a few minutes intentionally ushering participants over the bridge and set the stage for the purpose of the meeting, participants feel welcomed, acknowledged, prepared, and focused.

There are several aspects to consider when thinking about the bridge into your meeting and how best to bring participants across it. First, consider the climate of the group. As you remember from Chapter 5, climate refers to the feelings, beliefs, and perceptions people have in a group. Is the climate of this group a positive one? Do members feel valued, included, and heard? Is there a sense of emotional safety and trust? If the answer is no to any of these questions, you will need to address the climate at the beginning of the meeting either directly or in some other way. When there is a lack of sense of safety or inclusion, participants will not be able to fully participate or to participate productively.

A second consideration when bridging into your meeting is whether there are outside issues or contexts that need to be acknowledged. As I write this, we have come through a period of significant local, national, and international struggle, including a global pandemic, racial justice protests in response to violence and killings, a contentious election, an attack on our nation's Capitol, and other occurrences that have impacted each of us in various ways. We have also had successes, joys, and sorrows within our local communities. When we start a meeting by acknowledging what is likely in the hearts and minds of our participants, we create connections with them, honor their experiences, and demonstrate that we are paying attention. Unless it is an issue that needs greater attention, once we have recognized the outside issue, and participants' feel that their current experiences have been acknowledged, usually we can then go on to addressing the topic and meeting goals at hand.

There is some research that suggests that when meeting facilitators start the meeting with mindfulness, focusing participants on the topic and experience at hand, there is greater participation and more productive outcomes (Birk 2020; Rupprecht et.al. 2019). While mindfulness is still an unfamiliar and uncomfortable concept for some, it means being conscious of and focusing one's awareness on the present moment. It means switching off autopilot, disconnecting from distractions, and focusing on what is within and before you. Facilitators can help participants to be mindful in a variety of ways, sometimes without calling it "mindfulness." Some facilitators begin board meetings by reading the school's mission statement and asking participants to think of one way they have recently experienced the mission. Board meeting facilitators could ask board members to consider their board values and think about how best they might "live" them during the meeting. And certainly, facilitators of boards who are comfortable with the concept of mindfulness can start meetings with a moment of quiet where participants are invited to consider why they are there, to visualize a positive outcome, or to use other types of grounding focus. The goal is to help participants shift from focusing on their external considerations and bring their attention fully to the current situation.

STEP 4: FACILITATING THE MEETING

Now that you have primed your meeting participants to engage with your meeting topic, helped them across the bridge from the outside world into the positive climate of your group, and invited them to focus on the task at hand, it is time to actually discuss/learn/engage/decide! Facilitating effective and productive meetings is both a skill and an art. There are many guides for effective facilitation that can help new facilitators with tricks and tools. Here we will touch on two areas that skilled facilitators need to attend to: group engagement, and managing challenging conversations. Other considerations facilitators need to pay attention to include the process of decision-making and fostering diversity of thought, discussed in Chapter 3.

Group Engagement

We often fall into the habit of conducting all (or the majority) of our meetings with the full group, asking questions and engaging in conversation with twelve, fifteen, or more participants. This practice can be effective in some situations, yet it typically is not an inclusive practice. General, large group discussions usually result in full participation only by members who are extroverts and quick processors, or by those who have assumed or been assigned power and influence.

Members who prefer to think through ideas before speaking or who perceive that they have less power are frequently not heard in these situations. This can lead to bias—believing that you have consensus or a sense of the group's understanding based on the vocalization of a few, whereas others feel that they have not fully participated or been heard. It is therefore important to engage in group discussions and decision-making in ways other than only in a large group. There are many strategies meeting facilitators can use to engage people besides a large group. Many of the strategies that educators use in classrooms with students can be easily modified to be effective with adults:

- Small group discussions
- Round-robin responses (each person in the group responds)
- "World Café" (a process to engage
  small groups in considering big topics)
- Turn-and-talk (participants turn to their neighbors to discuss)
- Sticky notes on a "parking lot" (to capture
  thoughts that aren't spoken)

When thinking about the strategy or activity you will use to engage your group, start with the goal of the task. Meeting facilitators should develop a "tool kit" of various meeting facilitation strategies that they can pull from to accomplish a variety of purposes. In each situation, use or create a method of engagement that facilitates your group's interactions in order to accomplish your goals.

Challenging Conversations

In the board committee meeting I mentioned at the beginning of this chapter, the one that had little structure and was painful for me to attend, two of the participants got into an argument. They were both mature (over sixty-five), professional women, each of whom I knew to be kind, compassionate, and considerate. Both were strong-minded, and they butted heads. As a new member of the committee, I was uncomfortable with their exchange of terse, angry words. I didn't know the history of their relationship and wasn't sure if this type of interaction was common at these meetings. The committee chair did not help these two women with their disagreement; he let them argue, and when it seemed a good time to change the subject he did so without acknowledging that there had been an uncomfortable conversation. I wished he had recognized that they felt strongly about their positions, and had connected the discussion to our purpose and goals, establishing an intentional way to move forward productively. Instead, we all were left feeling as if there was no closure.

Any group that meets regularly will eventually experience conflict and differences of opinion. Conversations that are emotionally challenging for one or more people in the group will take place. How the group's facilitator navigates these challenging conversations will significantly impact the climate of the group: Are participants' opinions and feelings acknowledged, addressed, and processed, or are they shamed, attacked, or ignored? Effective facilitators carefully and intentionally set the stage for challenging conversations to occur by establishing the culture that allows participants to be honest and to fully engage. They then help participants navigate these conversations with respect and honesty. How to do this effectively is beyond the scope of this book, and is addressed by other researchers and writers. Nonetheless, in order to best serve their boards, board facilitators need to become aware of and competent in navigating challenging conversations.

STEP 5: ENDING THE MEETING

I recently attended a meeting where, as we approached the end of our scheduled time together, things began to speed up. We were on our last agenda item, yet hadn't fully addressed all the considerations.

The facilitator recognized that we were running out of time and started to talk more quickly. A participant, who didn't seem to notice the late hour, began speaking and there was a sense of impatience by others, as if they were thinking, *Hurry up! The meeting is almost over and we are done with all of this!* People became jittery and jumpy. As the concluding time arrived, the facilitator said in a rush, "OK, everyone, we need to end now, thanks so much—goodbye!" And we all left, somewhat flustered. We hadn't come to any conclusions about that last agenda item, we hadn't talked about preparation for our next meeting, we didn't assess how this meeting had gone, and we didn't acknowledge the good work we had just accomplished. Upon reflection, I realized that the meeting had actually been a very good one, but my perception of it was colored by how it ended.

The psychologist Hermann Ebbinghaus identified the "recency effect," a phenomenon that describes how we humans tend to remember the most recent things we have learned or experienced. If we have facilitated a productive and engaging board meeting, one where we engaged in strategic and generative discussions, navigated challenging conversations, made effective decisions, and were able to achieve our goals, and yet we ended the meeting in a rush without reflection or future planning (as so often happens), what memories and feelings are we leaving with our board members? How we end our meetings is as important as every other step in this process and, like every other step, can impact group climate as well as the achievement of goals. Carefully planning this step will result in participants feeling satisfied, accomplished, and prepared for what comes next.

There are three parts to ending a meeting: 1) summarizing what you have accomplished, 2) evaluating your effectiveness, and 3) planning for next steps. This phase of ending your meeting doesn't need to take significant time, although ensuring you have enough time to accomplish each part is important.

Start by summarizing your accomplishments, which can be done by highlighting decisions or plans made. This forms the basis of any minutes that will be crafted. Participants can add color or perspective to the list of accomplishments.

Evaluating the effectiveness of each meeting provides valuable information that can be responded to immediately. Facilitators might create an "exit ticket" for each member to complete that asks them to respond to prompts such as "I was aware of the goals for this meeting," "I received the information I needed to be fully prepared for this meeting," "We accomplished our goals for this meeting," and "Please list ways we could improve our future meetings." These types of prompts could also be sent electronically after the meeting (although in my experience, electronic participation after the meeting is lower than on paper immediately following a meeting). This is a simple yet powerful technique for learning about your meeting participants' experiences.

The final aspect of closing your meeting is planning for next steps. This is where you clarify who will do what, and by when. You can reiterate what each committee will be addressing at their next meeting and what they will share in their next report. This action planning supports board leaders in planning for the next full board meeting.

Facilitating carefully planned, well-managed, outcome-focused meetings is the most effective way board leaders can ensure they are making strategic decisions for their school. These types of meetings take time, planning, and effort to achieve. Board leaders who are disciplined and intentional about how they plan and facilitate meetings, and who take into consideration culture and climate, minimizing bias, the decision-making process, and strategic thinking when planning meetings will find that board members are more engaged, better prepared, and more effective in accomplishing the work of the board.

QUESTIONS TO ASK YOUR BOARD

Do our meetings have a specific, articulated purpose—every time?

Are all participants fully engaged in each meeting?

Is the climate of our board meetings positive? Is the climate of the meeting acknowledged and addressed?

Is diversity of thought supported and facilitated?

Do participants engage in challenging conversations in a respectful and constructive manner?

How might we change our agendas to facilitate more strategic meetings?

8

COMMITTEES
THAT WORK

Committees and task forces are the board's "divide and conquer" structure that allows board members to push key planning and tactical work forward and preserves full board meeting time for all members to come together for the more strategic work.

NAIS WEBSITE, "CREATE THE RIGHT BOARD
STRUCTURES AND PRACTICES: COMMITTEES"

The new head of school called me in the spring of 2019, and I could hear the exhaustion and frustration in his voice. This was his first headship and he was working feverishly to meet all the demands of the various school constituents. He felt good about the work he was doing with the faculty and he was bringing around the administrative team to be more collaborative and productive. The problem was the board. They were good-hearted people who were passionate about the school. They would do anything to support him and his efforts—which was the problem! They met so often and had such long meetings, he had no time to rest or think! He told me that he was scheduled to attend three committee meetings and a full board meeting all in that week. The board met monthly and there were seven standing board committees, some of which met weekly. He couldn't keep this up.

Committees are small groups of people who gather on a regular or time-limited basis to provide guidance, information, oversight, or resources to a larger body. We know from research and experience that we can accomplish work differently in smaller groups than larger groups (Gurteen n.d.). Committees provide the forum for small groups of people to think flexibly, hear all voices and viewpoints, and make thoughtful, strategic decisions. Committee work often provides the advance thinking, research, and considered options that larger groups can use to make final decisions.

It is very difficult, if not impossible, for a board of ten or more people to effectively conduct all of its work all together, even if they meet monthly. There is considerable discernment, research, and discussion that is needed in order to make the strategic decisions required of governing boards. Which is why boards usually form committees to accomplish much of this work. However, many board committees do not work efficiently and therefore, do not effectively support their board or their school. The most effective boards have 1) the right committees to effectively focus on and accomplish board goals, 2) committees that have clear charges and articulated goals, and 3) committees that run efficient meetings and maintain the culture and climate that allow for inclusive decision-making.

STANDING AND AD HOC COMMITTEES

There are two types of committees that boards can establish, each with important roles. Standing committees are those that meet regularly every year, and are often listed in the board's bylaws. Examples of standing committees are the finance committee and the governance committee. Ad hoc or task force committees are established to serve a particular need or accomplish a specific goal and are time-limited; ad hoc or task force committees are disbanded once the goal is accomplished. Examples of ad hoc or task force committees are a strategic planning committee (to support the development of the plan) and a bylaws review task force.

It is recommended that boards limit the standing committees they maintain to those that are essential to the ongoing work of the board. Having too many committees that do not serve specific, essential functions dilutes the efforts of board members and can be overwhelming to manage. Essential committees for small schools typically include:

- The finance committee, whose charge is to oversee the school's finances, lead the board in oversight and planning for financial sustainability, and ensure audit compliance

- The governance committee, whose charge is to recruit, orient, and mentor board members, oversee board leadership succession, and facilitate ongoing board professional development

- The head evaluation and support committee, whose charge is to provide professional and personal support for the head of school, support the development of the head's annual goals, and conduct the annual evaluation of the head of school (see Chapter 9)

- The executive committee, whose charge is to support the head of school in making decisions when the full board is not available

A note about the executive committee: It may not be necessary. Executive committees were constructed to conduct business in the event that the full board was unable to meet and there was urgent business to conduct. With technology the way it is today, this is less likely to occur and is rarely needed on a small board. Nonetheless, "some boards form an executive committee just because everyone else has one—it seems to exist by default" (BoardSource 2017). Some boards use an executive committee as a regular standing committee, often meeting to discuss and plan before every full board meeting. There are several problems that can occur with this practice. One is that there can be role confusion regarding who has authority and decision-making power. If the executive committee is doing much of the advance work that typically is conducted by other committees, what roles do committees play? This can also be undermining for the full board. Board members who are not on the executive committee may feel excluded from the important work of the board. And members who are on the executive committee, along with the board chair and the head of school, may experience feelings of burnout from having so many meetings to attend. BoardSource (2017) reminds us: "When creating any committee, it is wise to first analyze the entire structure of the board and determine whether that particular committee would add value."

In addition to the finance, governance, and head evaluation and support committee, there are other standing committees that small schools might find useful, such as:

- The advancement committee, whose charge is to coordinate and manage the development and fundraising activities of the board. This committee may also need to support the school's development and fundraising efforts if there is not sufficient school personnel. (See Chapter 12.)

- The assets committee (or buildings and grounds committee), whose charge is to support the stewardship of the school's assets

These last two committees actually are more operations-focused. Boards need to carefully consider if their schools need this type of support and work to maintain their focus on governance matters related to the topic as much as possible. If board involvement in development and fundraising or assets management is needed at the operations level, be clear that these activities are beyond the governance purview.

Many boards these days also have a DEIB or DEIJ (Diversity, Equity, Inclusion, Belonging and/or Justice) committee that focuses on issues related to diversity, equity, inclusion, belonging, and justice. There are differing thoughts about this. On the one hand, a DEIB committee may be very beneficial in supporting a board in thinking about these issues broadly and how it might improve its practices to be able to govern effectively. One the other hand, many people argue that all committees need to conduct their work with a DEIB lens and that establishing a stand-alone committee may enable board members to abdicate that work to the named committee. Once again, the most important thing a board can do is to be clear about the committee's charge. Is this committee focused on governance-level issues and topics that allow the board to think and plan for the future success of the school without delving into operations work? Will this committee hold all committees accountable for addressing diversity, equity, inclusion, and belonging?

Committees that are *not* recommended for independent school boards include a program committee, admissions or enrollment committee, or any other committee that focuses solely on operations. These invite board members to inappropriately "cross the line" into operations. There are appropriate ways for board members to engage in strategic thinking about program and enrollment (see Chapter 10); facilitating a standing committee is not one of them.

Establishing an ad hoc or task force committee is an effective and efficient way to accomplish a board's short-term goals. If the board needs to review and revise its bylaws, an ad hoc bylaws review committee can be established to do the work. During an accreditation self-study, it may be beneficial to have a committee that shepherds the board's engagement in self-reflection. These committees meet for a limited time to accomplish a specific goal and are disbanded once the goal is achieved so that board members can focus their efforts on other goals.

At the beginning of each school year the board leadership needs to facilitate the populating of committees. Ideally, each board member serves on one committee, although some boards members serve on two or more committees. Some boards allow board members to choose the committees on which they serve. In these boards, the board leadership (including the board chair and committee chairs) identifies the committees that will be needed for the upcoming year and shares this information with board members (often at the annual board retreat). They might include an overview of the committee's charges and any specific goals to be accomplished. Then board members can identify where they would like to serve. Other boards assign members to committees based on the board's needs. In any case, boards should establish a process for deciding who will serve on each committee and follow it regularly.

COMMITTEE WORK

Committees do the preparation and advance work that supports the full board to make well-considered and -researched decisions. In order to be most effective, committees need to maintain focus on a clear and shared purpose. Effective committee work is a result of careful planning and disciplined practices including establishing and working to achieve goals (Chapter 6) and facilitating effective meetings (Chapter 7). Committees can gather data, think through scenarios, and make recommendations; in essence, do the initial strategic thinking required to make good decisions (see Chapter 3). In other words, committees need to follow the effective practices recommended for the full board outlined in other chapters in this book.

Once committees have engaged in the initial strategic thinking regarding a topic, they need to facilitate the full board's strategic thinking. Committees can develop the materials to be sent to board members before a meeting and the questions that will guide board consideration during a full board meeting. This takes some of the responsibility off the board chair (and head of school) for developing all aspects of each board meeting agenda. In this way, committees take on some of the responsibility for ensuring that the board's goals are accomplished. The most effective boards have fully functioning committees that prepare members to make the best decisions.

QUESTIONS TO ASK YOUR BOARD

Do we have the standing committees that will fully
support the accomplishment of our board goals?

Do each of our committees have clear charges
and annual goals to guide our work?

Do our committees regularly prepare the full board
to engage in considered decision-making?

Do we form ad hoc or task force committees
to accomplish time-limited goals?

9

HEAD SUPPORT
& EVALUATION

---

*Because working well with the board is so central to the success
of both the head and the school, building a solid relationship is
worth every bit of the attention and thoughtfulness it takes.*

NORMAN COLB, *THE BOARD OF TRUSTEES—FRIEND, FOE, BOSS, OR PARTNER?*

I t was the end of the school year in 2010. Navigating our small
school through the global economic crisis over the prior couple
of years had been challenging, to say the least! I was finishing my third year as a head of school, and coming to the end of my
first contract. My primary accomplishment (other than transition-
ing the school from a founding head) was that I had managed to
keep the school open. Our enrollment had been a roller coaster ride,
we had unexpected building repairs, I was in regular meetings with
the bank about our mortgage, and I was still learning on the job how
to lead a school. And yet we were making our finances work, and our
parents, students, and faculty members were generally happy with
the school. I wasn't looking for or expecting any kind of special acco-
lades, and certainly not any monetary awards or bonuses; we had

frozen salaries for two years. The satisfaction of keeping our community together, when other small schools in my area had closed or were planning to close, was enough for me. So I was surprised when, at the end of our annual meeting in June, my board chair handed me an envelope and said it was a small token of appreciation from the board members to acknowledge my hard work. It was a gift certificate for a day at a local spa.

That gift was one of the kindest I have ever received. It was unexpected, heartfelt, and meaningful. I enjoyed the day at the spa, of course, but trite as it sounds, it truly was the thought that counted. My board recognized my work and the stress that work had produced, and offered acknowledgement and support in a meaningful way.

We talk in schools about educating "the whole child" and paying attention to their social and emotional needs as well as their cognitive and educational growth. And yet we often overlook the need to do the same for the adults in our buildings; to support the whole adult. When boards think of themselves as the employer of the head, they often focus on evaluation and feedback regarding performance, working to ensure the head is meeting expectations, goals, and standards. There is often less attention paid to support and growth. Yet, it is the board that is responsible for considering *all* of the needs of their one employee, the head of school.

Boards need to be attuned to both the personal and professional needs of the head of school not only because that person is their one employee, but also because the success or failure of the school rests on the head of school's performance. The head of a school directly impacts the ability of their school to survive and thrive. The board must therefore pay careful attention to 1) their own relationship with the head of school, 2) how the head of school is performing, and 3) how the head of school is feeling. Each of these will in turn impact the school. In my experience, boards sometimes struggle to understand the difference among these three types of support and how to provide them.

The relationship between the head of school and a board is an unusual one. The board is the employer, and hires, fires (if necessary), and evaluates the head. Yet the head of school typically has much more information about the organization, the field of education, and the role of governance than anyone on the board. In many small schools I've worked with, the question "Who manages the board?" comes up frequently. In the absence of a strong, knowledgeable board chair who can address the culture, climate, and efforts of the rest of the board, the head of school may need to take on a greater role in overseeing and facilitating the board's work. If this is necessary, part of what the head of school needs to do is to strengthen the board so that they can take back control of their own management. However, I have also worked with boards that have been disconnected from the head of school. The head was a recipient of information from the board rather than a partner. While this might work in some situations, this is not always the most effective relationship. The board and the head of school need to be in a balanced partnership, with each role clarified and understood, with close collaboration, and with respect and trust. The quality of this relationship is paramount, and both boards and heads of school should make it a priority to foster a positive partnership.

In a small school especially, with the close-knit community and people wearing "many hats," the head of school can become physically and emotionally exhausted. Given their role, there rarely is anyone within the school that the head of school can confide in or lean on; it is lonely at the top. Without intruding into their personal life, attuned boards can pay attention to the well-being of the head of school and either provide appropriate support themselves or facilitate the type of support that would be most helpful. Likewise, boards can and should be aware of the professional needs of the head of school. With limited budgets, small school heads often are not able to access the professional development or professional connection opportunities that other, better-resourced heads of schools have. Yet all professionals need to be "lifelong learners," especially educators! Boards need to consider the needs of their heads of school and creatively provide the support that will best enable them to thrive.

Some boards establish a Head Support and Evaluation Committee to focus specifically on these activities. This is a committee that is tasked with thinking about and supporting the personal and professional needs of the head of school as well as conducting assessments to support the head of school's evaluation. This structure works well in many situations, when roles are clearly defined and the head of school feels truly supported by the committee. If there is no committee to accomplish this work, the board chair will need to ensure that personal and professional needs of the head are addressed.

PERSONAL SUPPORT

How does an employer support the personal needs of their employee? Doesn't this inappropriately cross boundaries? In a small school, where the head of school is responsible for so many aspects of the running of the school and where the survival of the school can rest on how effective the head of school is in accomplishing those tasks, it is critical that the well-being of the individual is considered. Certainly, as boards consider the personal support they might provide for their heads of school, they need to keep in mind boundaries and be very careful that they do not intrude into the heads of schools' personal lives. Nonetheless, there are several specific ways that any employer can support an employee, and one that is more specific to boards. Independent school boards can and should consider how they support their heads of school in the following ways:

1 Ensuring the working conditions and expectations are conducive to mental, emotional, and physical wellbeing. This includes ensuring that pay and benefits are fair and consistent with those in the

immediate marketplace, there is sufficient leave and vacation time, job descriptions and expectations are clear and upheld, and job performance is evaluated, recognized and supported.

2 Actively and intentionally fostering a positive, collaborative, and respectful culture and climate.

3 Remaining in regular communication with your employee to understand what their perceptions and needs are. A head of school who does not feel supported and who feels significant stress, conflict, and concern, is not going to be able to fully fulfill their job responsibilities. While it is not the board's right to pry into a head's personal life, it benefits the school when the board, or at least the board chair, is aware of the head's feelings and provides desired support. A useful question to be asked regularly is, "What's keeping you up at night right now?"

4 Being as effective as possible in their role as governors. Boards put stress on their heads of school when they are ineffective or lack knowledge, as this requires the heads to step in and manage the boards.

PROFESSIONAL SUPPORT

In addition to supporting the head of school's personal well-being, the board also needs to support them professionally. Ensuring that the head of school has the knowledge, resources, and connections to be able to perform their leadership role in a way that best meets the needs of the school is in the best interest of the board. As with most aspects of board work, the place to start is with setting goals. What are the long-range and shorter-term goals of the school? What skills and abilities does the head of school need to

accomplish those goals? How can the board support the head of
school in acquiring or enhancing those skills and abilities?

In addition, boards can support heads of schools in their own
desired professional growth. What competencies do they themselves want to learn or enhance? Establishing a professional growth
plan with the head of school that identifies specific outcomes will
provide clarity and focus for both the head of school and the board.
This growth plan can establish what the board wants the head of
school to accomplish and what the head of school wants to accomplish. Then, together, they can identify how they will accomplish
this growth. The board will then need to ensure that the school
financially supports the head's professional growth by funding the
professional development. Some learning avenues for a head of
school's professional growth include:

1 Professional development courses, workshops, and other
   training opportunities offered by associations and others
2 Academic classes at a university
3 A personal learning project (carefully planned)
4 Work with an individual or group coach or mentor
5 Volunteering outside of the school, such as serving on another
   organization's board or serving on an accreditation team

Paying attention to the personal well-being and professional
growth of their heads of school is often not what rises to the top
of the list when boards think about what is important or urgent
to address. And yet these are critical considerations and responsibilities of an independent school board. A school will not thrive if
its head of school is not fully able to perform their duties, either
because they are exhausted and overwhelmed or because they do
not have the skills and competencies necessary to address the challenges at hand. Effective boards ensure that their heads of school

are fully supported to perform their duties with the highest level of efficacy possible.

ASSESSMENT AND EVALUATION

In addition to reflecting on how the board interacts with the head of school, and providing the support needed for their head of school to be the best leader possible, boards have a responsibility to provide honest, clear, and timely feedback regarding their perceptions of the heads of schools' performance. This proves difficult for many boards for a variety of reasons. Board members often don't fully understand all that the head of school does or know exactly what to assess. And they often don't have an easy, cost-effective tool for evaluating the head.

People confuse the concepts of assessment and evaluation. They are similar and intertwined yet describe two different parts of a process to measure achievement, efficacy, and success. Assessment is the measurement of discrete skills, abilities, and, at times, opinions. A math test is an assessment. Evaluation is an act of making a judgment about someone or something. People often make evaluations of performance based on a series of assessments. A math grade at the end of the term is an evaluation of performance or achievement.

These distinctions are important to understand when considering how to measure and give feedback regarding job performance. Too often we make judgments (evaluations) about performance with little or no assessment of actual performance. This leaves us open to bias and error.

Each independent school board needs to consider how it will evaluate its head of school each year to make the determination or judgment that the head of school continues to meet the needs of the school and also to determine what goals to set for the upcoming year or years. To be able to do this, board members first need to understand what the head of school actually does on a regular basis. The majority of this is articulated in a job description (with an understanding there is much that is subsumed under "other duties as necessary"). Board members need to be familiar with the head of school's job description and, in collaboration with the head of school, should ensure that it accurately reflects their duties as they are able. I don't believe any job description can fully articulate all the roles and responsibilities that a person accomplishes in their job, yet it is important to have as accurate a job description as possible. In addition to the job description, there are other standards against which a board can assess the head of school's performance. These standards can be general, and come from an outside organization such as NAIS or ISM, or they can be internal, generated by the board or the head of school. Boards can also gather opinions from school constituents about the head of school's performance. Here are four common performance assessments:

1 *Measurement of achievement of predetermined general performance goals or competencies* These might be from a job description or set of standards created by another organization such as NAIS or ISM.

2 *Measurement of achievement of pre-determined personally developed goals* These are the goals developed collaboratively by the head and board at the beginning of the year.

3 *Opinion about general performance offered by the board, staff, parents, and students* This is what is typically referred to as a "360 review."

4 *Self-evaluation* Often this is a narrative written by the head regarding their own opinion of what they have accomplished.

It is important to remember that these types of assessments serve dual purposes of providing the head of school with the information needed in order to grow and the board with the information needed to evaluate and supervise.

Assessments of the head of school do not need to look the same every year. A new head of school will need more targeted and frequent assessment of performance and feedback than a more experienced head of school needs. Once a head of school is established, after serving in the role for several years, many schools move to a rotating system of evaluation. They may assess and provide feedback on annual goals every year but only conduct a full 360 assessment by the community every three years. Boards and heads of school can work collaboratively to establish what information will be helpful to each, when it would be beneficial to have the information, and how the different types of information will be used.

At the end of each year, once the assessment data has been collected, the board needs to identify how they will evaluate and provide feedback to the head. Some boards use an evaluation measurement scale such as "Exceeds Expectations, Meets Expectations, Does Not Meet Expectations," similar to the types of evaluations we provide for students. Other boards are not as formal and simply provide a summary of the assessments collected. In either case, boards will need to be intentional and thoughtful about the way they convey feedback to the heads. Conducting a meeting to specifically discuss the assessments and overall evaluation of the heads' performance indicates that this is an important endeavor and provides the opportunity for dialogue. If any corrective action is being suggested, this will need to be conveyed clearly and with supporting documentation. This feedback session can also be the time to begin the discussion about setting goals for the upcoming year.

The importance of the board's role in supporting, assessing, and providing feedback to the head of school about job performance cannot be overstated. This is a critical responsibility, and one that is not always accomplished with careful consideration. The head of school is the board's one employee, and the person responsible for ensuring the success of the school. Effective boards recognize that it is their responsibility to ensure that the head of school has all of the support, information, and professional development they need to perform at their very best.

QUESTIONS TO ASK YOUR BOARD

How do we as a board consider our relationship with the head of school?

Do we have a head of school evaluation and support committee of the board? If not, who is paying attention to the head of school's needs?

How does our board support the personal wellbeing of our head of school?

How does our board support the professional development and growth of our head of school?

Does our head of school have an accurate job description? Are board members familiar with this job description?

Does our head of school evaluation process meet the needs of our board as well as our head of school?

What assessments do we use to evaluate our head of school's effectiveness?

How often do we evaluate?

How do we provide feedback regarding evaluations?

How does our board use evaluation to support and supervise our head of school?

10

———

ENROLLMENT
& PROGRAM

———

As a Trustee . . . you make sure that board-generated policies
further the school's mission and lesson risks to the school and
its community through appropriate governance oversight
and assessment. You are the ultimate custodian of the school's
well-being, and you use your role in shaping, approving,
and monitoring policies as a tool to achieve this end.

MARY DEKUYPER, *TRUSTEE HANDBOOK: A GUIDE TO EFFECTIVE
GOVERNANCE FOR INDEPENDENT SCHOOL BOARDS*, 9TH EDITION

W hen I was a new head of school, eager to tell people
about my wonderful little school, I was often asked,
"What kind of school is this?" To explain, I would
launch into a long description of our intentionally small school
with hands-on learning, nurturing teachers, and an engaging curriculum. We weren't a Montessori school or a Waldorf school, but
we borrowed some of their philosophies and practices. Our fields
and playgrounds were a Certified National Wildlife Habitat, and
we used the outdoors as a classroom. We spent time outside every
day. Students had a sense of being well-known within the school
community, and learning was individualized. My response to the
question "What kind of school is this?" was long, convoluted, and
often focused more on what we weren't than what we were. It wasn't

a very compelling message. I realized that our school needed to be clearer about our mission and purpose in order to be able to effectively communicate what we offered. I began wondering if this might be a factor that was impacting our enrollment.

For most of the small schools I have encountered, enrollment is their number one concern; it is the issue that keeps heads of school and board members up at night and that they talk about most often in board meetings. Enrollment is the backbone of a school's financial structure, and in a small school, the gain or loss of a few students can be the difference between a balanced budget and a deficit budget. And with small classes, the loss of one or two students can start a domino effect and impact whether or not others stay. Schools want classes filled with "mission-appropriate" students, preferably with waiting lists to ensure those classes remain full. Yet, because many small schools are under-enrolled, the administration is forced to consider taking students who may not be the best fit for their school just to balance the budget. This is not an optimal situation to be in for a variety of reasons. When schools struggle to realize the enrollment that supports their business model, boards understandably feel the need to address the situation. Indeed, it is their responsibility to address it. However, they often go about it in unproductive ways.

Think about why parents are drawn to a school: They want a certain environment that will best meet their expectations and their child's needs (Torres 2019). In order to find the right school for their children, parents need to know which schools provide the programs that will meet those expectations and needs. There are many vehicles parents use to find out about schools, and schools must use effective marketing strategies to communicate their missions and programs. Yet how do you know what to say in your marketing campaign if you don't have a coherent and well-articulated mission and purpose, as was true at my school? And how do you know which parents to market to; which families are looking for what your school has to offer?

The schools that have the most stable and enduring enrollments are those that have *mission-program-message-market* alignment. These schools are crystal clear about what they offer and whom they serve. Their mission is more than just a statement—it is a comprehensive purpose, deeply understood by all in the community. There is congruence between the mission of the school and the programs, pedagogy, and curriculum offered by the school. In essence, the mission is "lived" everyday in every aspect of the programming. The story of this congruence between the mission and the program is easily told through the variety of marketing messages that are conveyed both internally and to the external world. And there is a market for these schools' missions; there are families who have the interest and the means to enroll their children. Schools that have alignment between their mission and program, and that are able to communicate this alignment to the right market, are the schools with enrollments that are able to fully support their business models.

Once I realized that my own school was out of alignment between its mission and program because our mission was unclear, I was able to work with my board on addressing the problem. We considered a variety of ways to clarify our mission and, in the end, decided to become an International Baccalaureate Primary Years Program World School. Not all schools need to connect to a larger organization such as the IB in order to clarify their mission; in fact, most schools do not do this. It was what was right for our school, though, as the IB programming was similar to what we already provided. Other schools might simply need to better articulate the essence of their purpose and then translate this into how they provided their programming and services. For our school, adopting an IB framework allowed us to align our program with a clear purpose. This in turn helped us revamp our marketing campaign and target families in our area who would be interested in and benefit from our inquiry-based teaching and programming. It took several years to get all these pieces in alignment (which included training teachers, purchasing new curricula, and various marketing campaigns) but we accomplished it. As our enrollment numbers went up and our attrition rate went down, I became more and more confident that we had a strong mission that was lived daily in our program.

What was the board's role in all of this? Their job was to help me, collaboratively, to set the policies around all these decisions and changes. Prior to this change in our mission, the board had spent many meetings considering our school's enrollment and brainstorming ways to improve it. They admitted that our school was the "best-kept secret" in the county and planned ways to get the word out. They framed the problem from an admissions standpoint and considered it from a variety of perspectives, yet remained focused on tactical, operational problem-solving. Once they shifted their focus off immediate enrollment, and began looking at the bigger picture of our school's *mission-program-message-market* alignment, change took place. When the board leaves current enrollment to the head and administration, they can then turn their attention to questions such as "What are the demographic data in the zip codes where the majority of our students live projected to be over the next three to five years?" and "What attrition percentages are we comfortable with, and what numbers will trigger closer investigation and intervention?" A board's job is not to fix enrollment; it is to set policy to create, and hold the head accountable for, the conditions that ensure stable enrollment.

Boards can use the strategic thinking process (outlined in Chapter 3) to consider, strategize, and plan for the programmatic and enrollment health of the school. First, clearly articulate your goal. Consider the factors that impact enrollment and if you are in full alignment across *mission-program-message-market*. What is it that you need to focus on and change? Next, think about and analyze what you know or think you know about your situation or issue. What misconceptions might you be holding? This will lead you to understand what data would be helpful to collect. Once you have collected and considered data, you can develop options for addressing your situation or issue. Before deciding upon a course of action, consider each option from a variety of perspectives.

GENERATIVE QUESTIONS BOARDS CAN ASK

Here are some specific, generative questions boards can ask about their *mission-program-message-market* alignment to help identify goals:

Mission

- Do our current foundational statements (such as mission, vision, values, "we believe," and guiding principles) accurately and fully convey our mission?
- Do we see our mission reflected in everyday programming? How and where?
- What might threaten our ability to maintain our mission?

Program

- What evidence do we have that our programs reflect and "live" our mission?
- How can we measure how well our programs reflect our mission?
- What might threaten our programs' ability to reflect our mission?

Message

- Are we clear about all the ways we are messaging to the world about our school?
- Are our messages consistent across platforms?
- Do our messages accurately convey our mission and programs?
- What might threaten our ability to message accurately?

Market

- Do we have a clearly targeted market?
- Are there enough people in our market to support our school? How do we know?
- Are we sure that our market wants our mission?
- What might threaten our market and their interest in our school?

When board members spend their time talking about the details of current enrollment, they miss the opportunity to fulfill their role as strategic thinkers, focusing on the long-term health of the school. Board members need to be looking at the big picture of a school's mission and program and considering the factors, threats, and opportunities that may impact how their intended market views the congruence between mission and program. Of course, to be able to do this they need information about current enrollment and programming, and the head of school should be tasked with (and held accountable for) sharing enrollment and attrition details in ways that will inform more strategic discussions. Boards can then use this information to set policies, ask questions, and plan for the future health of their schools.

QUESTIONS TO ASK YOUR BOARD

Are we careful to focus on big-picture aspects of enrollment and program and leave the day-to-day management to the head of school and administration?

Are we considering the best questions about the long-term threats and opportunities to our enrollment and programs?

Are we addressing *mission-program-message-market* alignment?

Are we appropriately holding our head of school accountable for providing us with the information we need regarding current enrollment that will allow us to focus on long-term sustainability?

11

FINANCIAL FORESIGHT

Trustees must set policies to ensure the financial soundness of the school's assets and monitor the application of these procedures.

ISM, *BETTER BOARDS, BETTER SCHOOLS: THE ISM GUIDE FOR PRIVATE SCHOOL TRUSTEESHIP AND STRATEGIC GOVERNANCE*

I have a confession to make: Numbers are not my strong suit. Although I had some successes in math classes throughout my early education, I was one of the multitudes of students who left school feeling like I wasn't very good at math (even though that wasn't true). This gut feeling has followed me and sometimes makes my eyes glaze over when people start talking about numbers, budgets, and accounting. That feeling was with me when I served on my first board of a small school before I was a head of school; I didn't really understand the financial reports that were presented at each meeting. Sure, I could see when columns ended with positive or negative numbers, but I didn't fully grasp what each different report represented and what I, as a board member, was supposed to *do* with the information. It seemed like everyone else understood—no one

159

was asking for clarification—so I kept quiet and tried to participate as best I could.

What happened in those board meetings, and what I have seen happen in other boards, is that a lack of full understanding of financial reports by many board members, combined with lack of clear guidance by board leadership, stymies strategic or productive conversations. We tend to focus on the small details that make sense to us, that seem urgent, but that actually don't really matter in the end, when considering the big picture. I call this focusing on paperclips. The board doesn't need to weigh in on how much the school is paying for paperclips! Yet, in the absence of a structure that provides us with the information and the prompts to make more impactful decisions, we need to feel like we are doing something—so we focus on paperclips.

Small schools, with their lean budgets that are influenced by even minor fluctuations in enrollment, annual giving, or expenses, are frequently faced with immediate financial challenges. Balancing a small school budget typically requires vigilance, responsiveness, and creativity. The finances of a small school are at the center of most discussions and decisions that a board makes, as being a fiduciary for the school's financial sustainability is one of the board's primary responsibilities. And yet many small school boards focus *only* on the day-to-day finances without spending significant time considering and planning for the longer-term financial sustainability of the school. The urgency of the school's current financial standing, combined with lack of knowledge and guidance on how to think strategically, all combine to keep small school board members focused in a way that prevents them from being fully effective or fully successful.

An independent school board must focus on both *financial oversight* (overseeing the current financial standing of the school) as well as *financial foresight* (predicting and planning for the future). These two activities are, of course, intertwined and inform one another. Financial oversight includes approval of a budget for the upcoming year and ensuring that the previously approved, current budget is being appropriately managed, as well as overseeing and maximizing ongoing fundraising. Guidance and feedback regarding current budgets are appropriate from informed board members, but the management of these budgets is the responsibility of the administration. Effective boards spend the majority of their time with a financial foresight lens that includes establishing and managing a long-term strategic financial plan, ensuring that funds are being appropriately managed (that is, are invested wisely), and maximizing development efforts to cultivate long-term and future donors.

Included in financial oversight and foresight are tasks such as tuition-setting, financial aid policies, investment policies, and grant seeking. These are complicated and sometimes controversial topics for decision-making. The problem is that many board members do not have the financial understanding to be able to fully engage in deep consideration regarding the nuances of these topics. And board leadership often does not provide the resources or the processes that will allow them to actively contribute.

What I typically see in a small school boardroom is this: In the fall, the finance committee considers a budget presented by the head of school and/or business manager/CFO. Usually, boards have members on their finance committees with some financial acumen, so there is a good chance that they understand these documents. They work with the head of school and CFO to create a final draft of the budget, and then present it to the board. The budget is (often, but not always) sent out in advance of the board meeting, and board members are asked to review it before the meeting. At the board meeting, the chair of the finance committee asks the board members if they have any questions about the budget. After some discussion about specific line items, there is a request for approval and the budget is approved. Board members feel that they have accomplished their fiduciary responsibility for overseeing the financials of the school. But have they really?

Could those individual board members defend their decisions? Do they really understand what factors impact this budget? Did they consider alternatives or how this particular budget fits into the larger financial plan? Typically, the answer is no.

Consider the alternative: In early fall, the finance committee meets to discuss and update the strategic financial plan, which presents an overview of the school's finances for the next several years. They take into account the current year's enrollment and tuition, the known state of the economy, the area demographics, their local school competition, and their recent and planned development and fund-raising activities in order to establish a financial forecast for the next five years. From this forecast, they can identify the "levers" that will impact the upcoming school year's budget such as expected re-enrollment, projected new enrollment, financial aid, salaries and benefits, other costs, and fundraising yield expectations. Before the next board meeting, they share this high-level strategic financial plan along with a presentation (in graphic or dashboard form) of the levers for the upcoming school year. When they send out these reports, they ask board members to consider one or two questions before the meeting such as, Which of these levers is the most important to you and why? Are there other levers to consider that we have overlooked? What might threaten the assumptions you see in this strategic financial plan? Then, during the meeting, the board members break into small groups to share thoughts about these questions and then report back to the big group. The finance committee, head of school, and CFO use this feedback to guide their development of the next year's budget. When it is presented to the board at the next meeting, members have already considered the underlying assumptions and can approve it with a greater level of understanding.

So what is required to enable your board to have the knowledge, resources, and structure to be able to make strategic and productive financial decisions?

1 Regular training about the types of financial documents (see below) that schools use to manage and report on their financial standing. Remember that these reports are not intuitive for many people. Also, remember how adults learn: It is not through one-and-done presentations. Board members will need thoughtful, repetitive guidance on what these reports represent and how they are used.

2 Consider what information should be shared regularly in order for your board to be fully informed. Consider both the internal and external factors that impact your current and future finances. Boards do not need to know all the minute details to be able to make strategic decisions.

3 Consider how you share financial information to ensure it is clear, understandable, and leads to decision-making and action. Streamlined dashboards with visuals are helpful.

4 Create and follow an annual plan for considering financial standing. This was discussed in Chapter 6 on goal setting.

5 Identify how you will engage board members in meaningful discussions about finances. As discussed in Chapter 7, careful preparation will enable more strategic conversations.

FINANCIAL DOCUMENTS

In order to make informed, strategic decisions, it is crucial that board members have a deep understanding of the financial position of the school. However, accounting documents and financial reports are challenging for many people to understand, as they use a language that not everyone is familiar with and that is not intuitive for all. To enable board members to fulfill their fiduciary responsibilities, as well as maximize each board member's ability to fully contribute to financial discussions, board leadership needs to ensure that board members understand the types and purposes of each of the financial reports that are used by the school. These include the budget, profit and loss statement, cash flow statement, balance sheet, audit, and Form 990.

The first step that boards need to take when helping board members understand financial documents is to acknowledge that many board members have never seen a budget report before, and even if they have, don't fully understand how it is constructed. When I first became a board member, and even when I started my headship, I didn't really understand the difference between a profit and loss statement, a balance sheet, and the 990 form. I was confused when our cash flow and bank statement showed little money in the bank when our overall budget showed a (relatively) significant surplus. It took me a while (and a course on educational finance) to fully understand the data that each of these reports presented.

When board members are confused about finances, one must remember the following:

1 They will probably not let you know they are confused. These are adults who have been recruited to be knowledgeable governors. No one wants to appear ignorant in front of their peers.

2 They will focus on and talk about what they do know. Most people can understand the bottom line of a basic budget or profit and loss statement. They can see income in relation to the money going out. And they can comment on this.

Board leadership should be proactive and assume that most board members need training on board financial documents. Establish a method of training and provide it for all new board members as part of their orientation. You may have a video made by your CFO or auditor, create a handbook on financial documents, or offer outside training for board members. Then, regularly refer back to aspects of the training throughout the year. By ensuring that your board members have the necessary knowledge about board financial reports, rather than assuming that they already know, you will best prepare them to be able to participate in financial discussions.

FINANCIAL INFORMATION

When identifying the information your board needs in order to be fully informed, consider both internal and external data. Internal data are those indicators of the strength and health of internal school factors. External data are those indicators of the wider community factors that may directly impact your school.

Internal Factors

NAIS suggests the following basic areas that boards need to consider on a regular basis (NAIS 2011):

- Operating budget
- Operating cash flow
- Admissions pipeline
- Endowment and debt
- Physical plant
- Student turnover
- Financial aid
- Tuition
- Net tuition revenue
- Faculty
- Fundraising
- Staffing

External Factors

The above list of areas that board members need to be regularly aware of is primarily internally focused and has to do with the inner operations of the school. However, in an article in *Independent School* magazine, John Lewis argues that this set of data is not enough. "By only focusing on the internal microeconomic factors affecting the school and ignoring outside forces like demographics, the dashboard offered limited utility for decision-making and evaluating school performance" (Lewis 2020). He suggests that schools add external data to dashboards that are regularly or periodically shared with board members (and other stakeholders) including these factors:

- Current and future trends in total area population
- School-age population
- Median household income
- K–12 spending per student
- The percentage of students enrolled in private schools
- Inflation
- Employment
- Housing
- Peer industry trends
- Interest and exchange rates
- The stock market
- Consumer confidence

School board finance committees, in collaboration with the head of school and business officer/CFO, have the responsibility to carefully consider both the internal and external factors that impact the school's finances. Then they need to share the information with the full board. Taking into account and regularly considering all the factors that impact their school's financial health, both internal and external, will enable boards to provide the best oversight and foresight for the school.

DASHBOARDS

Once a board has identified the factors they want to regularly track that impact the school's short-term and long-term finances, then it must identify a reliable source for obtaining metrics related to each of those factors and create a method for sharing those metrics. Dashboard reports are used to convey the most important information in a clear and understandable way. Think of the dashboard of your car and the dials and indicators that let you know about the health and maintenance needs of your vehicle. You can look at the dashboard and quickly get a sense of how much gas you have, your oil levels, the temperature of the engine, and other important information. This is what your board needs, a set of data that they can use to be able to knowledgeably discuss the state of the school and then to make decisions. Summarizing data into easily understandable graphics, charts, and tables enables board members to fully understand what is being presented and also helps target discussions on specific topics. There are several examples of how to create dashboards of summarized data, such as NAIS's *The Trustee Dashboard* (NAIS 2011). Many boards create their own dashboard. And there are consultants who can help boards effectively develop dashboards. The key is to identify *what* needs to be shared and then *how* best to share it.

ANNUAL FINANCIAL PLANNING

The process for short-term and long-term financial planning needs to be clearly articulated and understood by each board member. As was discussed in the section on goal setting and planning in Chapter 6, identifying how and when the finance committee and the full board will consider each aspect of the school's finances each year is important to establish and follow. This supports the overall planning for the board, allows board members to understand and anticipate the annual calendar, and holds committees and board members accountable.

Annual planning can include:

- When the finance committee will update
  the strategic financial plan
- When the finance committee will update the next year's annual
  budget and when they will present its documents to the full board

Finance committees should also consider and plan for more periodic tasks, such as when to consider, update, and/or develop an investment policy, review the tuition-setting process and financial aid policy, and develop a salary plan. Planning for these activities ensures they will occur.

MEANINGFUL DISCUSSIONS ABOUT FINANCES

Informing board members about financial reports, identifying necessary information, creating a set of dashboard reports on the most important factors impacting school finances, and planning your conversations all prepare you for engaging board members in meaningful, strategic conversations about financial standing and sustainability. Now, you need to carefully plan and structure those conversations. Presenting a set of data and asking, "What do you think?" will rarely lead to focused, outcome-based conversations and decision-making. Rather, go through the processes outlined in Chapter 3 and Chapter 7. Start by establishing goals for what needs to be decided (such as tuition-setting, financial aid policies, new revenue sources, or whatever is most important for your board). Then consider what you think you know, what data you need, how you can consider various perspectives, and the various options before you. Determine what information board members will need to inform their thinking and when and how to get this information to them. Develop processes such as small group discussion, brainstorming sessions, design-thinking (where you first consider the desires and expectations of the consumer), or other methods for facilitating thinking, discussion, testing assumptions, and decision-making. Remember to allow substantial time for this process, as good decision-making takes time.

Effective boards take the time and engage in the planning necessary to ensure that their board members have the knowledge, resources, and structures necessary to make informed, strategic financial decisions. This is a process that can and should start at a board member's orientation. Boards that pay attention to how adults learn and process information (over time) and who intentionally support financial literacy, learning, and growth will enable their members to fully participate and be able to provide meaningful contributions to both financial oversight and foresight for their schools.

QUESTIONS TO ASK YOUR BOARD

How do we ensure that board members understand the different finance reports that our board uses to guide our financial decisions?

What are the internal and external factors that impact our finances?

What metrics can we use to measure the internal and external factors that impact our finances?

How can we summarize the data regarding the internal and external factors that impact our finances?

Are we spending too much time on either financial foresight or oversight?

What questions do we need to ask ourselves regarding current financial standing and regarding our future financial sustainability?

12

DEVELOPMENT & FUNDRAISING

Plan your fundraising strategy around the notion that your purpose is to ensure a better school 10, 20, and 30 years from now: The schools with the strongest and most enduring philanthropic cultures invite their constituents not to fix problems but to fund dreams.

ELIZABETH KOLB FARR, *THE IMPORTANCE OF FUNDRAISING STRATEGY*

The first time I was asked to participate in fundraising for a school, I agreed out of a sense of obligation, not out of eagerness or enthusiasm. I was working as an educator at my alma mater, and was "strongly encouraged" to help out with the school's fundraising efforts. We received some training that I thought (at the time) was fairly well done. It focused on connecting with potential donors to share with them positive aspects of the school before asking them to contribute to the annual fund. As an outgoing person, I thought that seemed relatively easy, and also an opportunity to connect with former classmates. Yet once I started making phone calls, I reverted to feeling uncomfortable about asking for money. It felt disingenuous to call folks out of the blue, chat for a while, and then ask them to send a check. Fortunately, as I moved into board service and later into headship, I received even more training and support in understanding the rationale supporting development and fundraising, and these activities no longer feel uncomfortable. I learned to shift my thinking about fundraising and I learned strategies for developing relationships with people to cultivate future donors. Now I consider providing others with the opportunity to contribute to and support an organization they care about as a gift, and it is an activity I engage in enthusiastically.

A pair of myths that many people still hold regarding board service is that you either need to have a lot of money to donate to the school, or you need to raise a lot of money. The first myth is connected to the old saying that organizations needed "time, talent, or treasure" or "work, wisdom, or wealth" on their boards, with heavy emphasis on treasure or wealth. While having generous people on your board who are willing to provide substantial financial support to the organization is certainly a good thing, focusing solely on a potential board member's ability to give or get is no longer wise for a variety of reasons. Rather, boards need to seek a diversity of members who bring the experiences and perspectives needed to accomplish their goals. Effective, modern boards move away from the siloed and limited adages of board members with "time, talent, or treasure" or "work, wisdom, or wealth," and consider how individuals can add to their board and school in meaningful and significant ways (see Chapter 4).

This is not to say that an independent school's board members don't have a responsibility for donating to the school—they do, and this expectation needs to be made clear from the very beginning. All board members should be expected to participate in annual giving and to give as generously as they are able. Many suggest that the school should be one of a board member's top three philanthropic recipients. Some schools make suggestions regarding minimum contributions, while others trust that board members will give at the level they are able. It is critical for other fundraising efforts that a school can attest that they have 100% participation by their board, so this giving expectation needs to be explicit.

My experience is that for most board members, they can accept that they will be expected to give an annual donation to the school; they are willing to give. The greater issue is the second myth: that board members will be expected to engage in a significant amount of fundraising. If you are like me, you may have approached fundraising with a variety of feelings: anxiety, fear, even loathing. Following my initial foray into fundraising, I was quick to tell people, "I don't like asking others for money." In my mind, fundraising felt intrusive, disrespectful, or sleazy. It certainly made me feel uncomfortable, and I used to avoid it whenever possible. Nonetheless, I have shifted my perspective and think about fundraising differently now. I started by considering my own giving; there are several organizations to which I give money, and others to which I give my time (by volunteering). When I think about *why* I give to these organizations, and how I feel about giving, it is disconnected from the feelings I listed above. When I give it makes me feel good, helpful, and generous. I don't begrudge these organizations for asking me to contribute; I am actually grateful for the opportunity. While certainly there are organizations that are irritating in their efforts to raise money, and we can learn from them what *not* to do, fundraising can be approached as providing an opportunity rather than intrusive pestering. In addition, there are many aspects of fundraising that do not involve directly asking someone for money. When board members shift their own perspectives and understand the dynamics of fundraising, they will be better able to support their schools.

There are different philosophies regarding the role of fundraising in sustaining an independent school's financial position. There are some who believe that a school's budget should rest solely on "hard income" that is raised through tuitions and other programmatic fees.

Others believe that regularly including "soft money," raised through fundraising and other development activities, is important in keeping tuitions lower and developing a culture of philanthropy that will be needed over time. In an effort to maintain affordability, these schools recognize a gap between what tuition covers and the actual costs of the school and bridge this gap with income raised through fundraising. Many independent schools in the US rely on fundraising to balance their budgets. They have a line item in their budgets and strategic financial plans for expected donations and count on this soft money to cover annual costs. Meeting annual giving goals is imperative to the financial sustainability of these schools.

ADVANCEMENT, DEVELOPMENT, AND FUNDRAISING

Let's talk about the terms *advancement*, *development*, and *fundraising*, as these are often used interchangeably. For many, all of these terms relate to raising money for the school. I think of them as relating to the financial sustainability of the school, yet each with a slightly distinct focus. Schools often define these differently than I do here, which is fine; I offer these distinct definitions to help board members think about how they organize their school support efforts.

- Advancement is the overarching activity of advancing the school through communications, marketing, external collaborations and partnerships, "friend-raising," and fundraising. Folks who work in advancement often help to coordinate all these activities.

- Development can be thought of as "friend-raising," or connecting with people and organizations who might be able and willing to support the school in some way in the future. Development includes donor cultivation, business partnerships, alumni relations, local community connections, etc. It includes

all the activities that can eventually lead to a request for
monetary, "in-kind," volunteer, or some other type of support.

- Fundraising is the actual raising of money by directly
  asking (such as annual funds or capital campaigns), and
  other activities that bring in cash or other resources
  (such as annual auctions or sales of goods). Development
  supports fundraising, yet is a different set of activities.

Many (if not most) small schools do not have the personnel to
support an advancement department and may have only one or two
administrators who are responsible for all of the school's advance-
ment/development/fundraising activities. Therefore, a school's board
needs to support the school administrators who are doing this work.
This will look different in each school, based on the configuration of
personnel and the school's goals. In some cases, where there is not a
school administrator in charge of development and fundraising, the
board will need to take a more active role in creating and managing development and fundraising plans. When there is a paid staff
member overseeing these activities, the board can take a more supportive role. In either case, being clear about goals and expectations
will be key in enabling board members to work collaboratively with
school administrators to raise the friends and funds the school needs.
Yet many small school boards do not have a clearly articulated fundraising plan beyond facilitating an annual fund campaign and/or
hosting an annual fundraising event. Fundraising goals are set based on
what was raised the previous year without a thorough consideration
of what is needed and why. In short, these schools are not thinking
strategically about their fundraising efforts. Yet, like all other aspects
of board service covered in this book, fundraising needs to be strategic, intentional, and disciplined. Boards need to know why they are
fundraising, what they are fundraising for, as well as how and when

fundraising will occur. They need to understand all the steps in the school's fundraising strategy in order to make ongoing decisions and to choose where they will be most helpful and comfortable participating. When boards have a comprehensive and articulated fundraising plan with clear expectations, the processes are manageable, and it is a team effort, then they will be much more successful in their efforts.

THE BOARD'S ROLE IN DEVELOPMENT AND FUNDRAISING

The place to start with board member participation in development and fundraising is to make clear the expectation that each member will participate in some way. Board members need to participate in developing potential "friends of the school" and in asking for donations from those "friends." Yet many people don't know exactly how to do this in ways that feel authentic, comfortable, and that specifically support the goals of the school. Board members need clear guidelines and instructions regarding their expectations for development and fundraising, as well as support in accomplishing those expectations. A board development and fundraising plan will clearly articulate what is expected of each board member and can also provide suggestions and support. This board plan is not to be confused with the development and fundraising plan of the school. The board plan will certainly support the school's plan, but it focuses specifically on what board members will do and accomplish. A plan for the board's engagement in development will outline the connections the school wants board members to foster. These could include:

- Alumni and alumni families
- Local businesses that might benefit from what the school offers and that might donate money, time, or other resources
- Grantmakers

- Major donors within the school community and outside
  the community (who might be interested in the mission)
- Businesses with whom the school might partner to
  provide services (such as camps or aftercare)

Once these areas for connection are established, goals and strategies for sustaining them can be developed (see Chapter 6). These goals will be both short-term (one to two years) and longer-term (three to five years) and will take into account any initiatives the board has established in its current strategic plan. Are you planning a building project? Will you be establishing or increasing your endowment? Do you need to strengthen your alumni relations? Creating this development plan could be part of a larger strategic planning process, or it could be developed on its own. Once established, board members can take on assignments and responsibilities as they feel comfortable and where they will have the most impact.

A plan for the board's engagement with fundraising has aspects that target annual activities as well as longer-term focus over the upcoming years. It will outline all the ways that board members will be involved in asking for money or other donations. These can include supporting the school's annual fund, other annual fundraising activities (auctions, festivals, sales), and specific major donor requests. Part of a board's fundraising plan should be to consider who might be major donors and how and when to engage with them. All members of the board can participate in considering who might be motivated to support the mission of the school with a large donation (large is any amount over your most generous annual fund donations). Then, with guidance from the development director (if you have one), you can make a plan that establishes who will communicate with potentially large donors, what the goal is, when the engagements will take place, and how you will express gratitude for participation and donations. Heeding the advice of experts in this area will be helpful; either by using your own employee, hiring a consultant, or at the very least, reading advice from expert authors about the process.

Understanding the different elements of development and fundraising is the first step; creating clear and comprehensive development and fundraising plans is the second step; and ensuring that each board member knows what their responsibilities are, and is held accountable for those responsibilities, is the third step in establishing effective methods for engaging board members in the critical work of financially supporting your school. Sometimes these steps seem overwhelming for a small school board. Yet they are extremely important; strategically creating these plans and engaging in this work needs to be a priority.

QUESTIONS TO ASK YOUR BOARD

Does our board have both a development and a fundraising plan?

Are board members made aware of our responsibilities regarding development and fundraising when recruited?

Are board members held accountable for our responsibilities regarding development and fundraising?

13

EVALUATING
THE BOARD

---

*In the end, you can't manage what you don't measure and you
can't improve upon something that you don't properly manage.*

LESLIE RIOPEL, *THE IMPORTANCE, BENEFITS, AND VALUE OF GOAL SETTING*

I t was the beginning of a strategic planning process for a small
school, and I was gathering information. I asked the board chair
if the board had evaluated itself in the past. She was quite pleased
to tell me that they did conduct an evaluation each year: Board members filled out a survey in the spring articulating how well the board
had done over the past year. She shared the results with me from the
prior two years. While I was happy that this board was taking the time
to assess itself—many boards do not—I recognized that they could
improve in this area. The survey questions primarily focused on
overarching and rather nebulous board tasks such as "The board has
adopted a clear statement of the school's mission, vision, and strategic
goals and has established policies and plans consistent with this statement" or "Board members understand the landscape and trends that

impact constituencies." While these questions have merit, and obtaining the understanding of board members regarding these aspects of governance might be interesting, I wondered how the school might use the responses to these questions. It seemed to me that there was much that was left off of the survey. There were no questions that assessed board members' opinions regarding the accomplishment of specific goals (set at the beginning of the year), or of aspects of governance that they could individually impact, such as whether they employed strategic thinking regularly. I wondered if the results of this very philosophically written survey might overwhelm the board—if they resulted in low scores, how would this help them? Would they know what they needed to change or improve? The point of assessing your board is to gain information that can help you identify strategies that will enhance and support your work moving forward.

What we measure is what we value, manage, and improve, as sayings go. If we value board efficacy and want to ensure that we are able to sustain strengths and address weaknesses within our ability to govern, we need to identify what we consider to be effective, and how to demonstrate whether our board is living up to our expectations. It is remarkable to me that schools, whose mission is focused on education—which typically includes assessment and evaluation—so frequently don't apply the measurement of learning and/or performance to the adults in the community. We spend a lot of time thinking and talking about how we measure student achievement and growth, but very little time thinking about how we measure the administration's or the board's achievements and growth. Boards in particular operate with minimal meaningful feedback regarding their efficacy.

There may be several reasons for this: In small schools, boards are so frequently caught up in the urgent that they overlook the important; they address the immediate crisis rather than considering longer-term performance. Also, there is not a lot of guidance regarding board assessment and evaluation. We are told evaluations need to be done, but not how to do them. There are organizations that will conduct board surveys and provide valuable feedback; however, many of these organizations provide only broad feedback rather than specific recommendations. And often those organizations charge a hefty fee to conduct those surveys, which challenges many small school budgets. Many boards, such as the one described at the beginning of this chapter, develop their own sets of questions for board members, yet unless they have someone with experience in writing survey questions, these may not be particularly robust. So often, boards are left adrift when it comes to assessing and evaluating their own performance. (See Chapter 9 concerning evaluating the head of school; *assessment* is the measurement of discrete skills, abilities, and at times opinions, while *evaluation* is an act of making a judgment about someone or something.)

Furthermore, boards may approach their own assessment and evaluation with anxiety. People fear that the process will be onerous, time-consuming, or costly; that there will be blame or shame; or that weaknesses will be highlighted that will be challenging to correct. Nonetheless, anxiety or fear is not sufficient reason to put off an evaluation process that will likely result in data that can help your board be more efficient and effective.

Regular assessment of the board will provide data that will be informative in a variety of ways. Assessments can reveal a number of things: how individual board members feel about their work and the efforts of others, the perceived efficacy of processes and procedures used, and the quality of the relationship with the head of school. Board assessments can reveal differences in the head of school's perspectives and those of board members, and uncover inefficiencies in processes, planning, and practices. Boards can consider the assessment data in order to identify what can be improved or changed regarding the focus of the board, the processes used to conduct committee and board meetings, the board member recruitment process, board professional development, and the culture and climate of the board. And then, if helpful, boards can use the assessment data to evaluate their overall effectiveness. A good assessment and evaluation process keeps the board accountable.

Many boards look outside of their schools to find assistance in assessing themselves. There are organizations (such as NAIS and ISM) that provide board assessment and evaluation tools along with a summary of the results. There are also consultants who will conduct board assessments and evaluations, and then provide more personalized recommendations. And some schools conduct their own board evaluations, with board member assessments that they have created themselves. Regardless of who is conducting the process, boards will be wise to consider who and what they assess, and how and when they evaluate.

WHO TO ASSESS

Assessments provide the data that support an evaluation or judgment of the overall efficacy of the board. Board member self-assessment is the most common method of gaining these data, and board members are the obvious group to query about their own efficacy and achievement. Nonetheless, boards will get more nuanced feedback if they also assess the board chair and the head of school separately, and consider those two sets of feedback in combination with feedback from board members. The board chair and the head of school have a wider view of the board with more information than board members. Therefore, it is beneficial to assess and consider three sets of feedback separately: 1) board members, 2) board chair, and 3) head of school.

Others outside of the board can also be surveyed to provide feedback regarding the work of the board. The more general, annual surveys that gather opinions from faculty, staff, parents, and alumni can include questions regarding the work of the board. Questions could include the following: Do community members understand the strategic priorities of the board? Are board members visible? Do community members have confidence that the board is governing effectively? Responses to these questions can be combined with the assessment data from board members, the board chair, and the head of school to support the overall evaluation of a board's work.

WHAT TO ASSESS

Typically, board members are asked to complete a survey focused on the accomplishments of the board as a whole, and the results are compiled and presented back to the group. The data from these self-assessments are valuable, and give important feedback regarding board members' feelings and opinions regarding the work of the board. However, if the questions are only targeting the overall work of the board, this one data set is not sufficient for a complete board evaluation. Boards will benefit from regularly assessing the breadth of areas they impact as governors. These include the work of 1) board as a whole, 2) the board chair, and 3) individual board members.

When considering the efficacy of the work of the full board, there are two overarching areas to assess: the achievement of specific annual goals and the achievement of regular board roles and responsibilities. The following are ten key areas that boards can assess in addition to assessing the accomplishment of specific goals. Underneath each area, there are sample questions that might be asked on an assessment that can provide information to support evaluation of the board's work as a whole:

1 *Board composition*
   • Do we have the board members we need to most effectively and productively accomplish our work?

- Does the board reflect the racial, ethnic, age, and economic diversity of our parent body?
- Do board members have the skills, abilities, and experience that our school needs (i.e. legal expertise, financial knowledge)?

2 *Board meeting process and procedures*
   - Are our board and committee meetings conducted in the most efficient way possible that allows us to effectively conduct our work?
   - Do board meetings generally start and end as planned?
   - Do members receive board reports and materials enough in advance to be read and absorbed before meetings?

3 *Board culture, climate, equity, and inclusion*
   - Do we have the culture and climate that allows each of us to feel included, welcomed, valued, and heard?
   - Do all board members feel valued and included?
   - Are differing perspectives welcomed and encouraged?

4 *Committee structure and processes*
   - Do our committee structure and processes allow us to fully and effectively complete our work?
   - Are there enough board members to support the work of our committees?
   - Do the committees that the board has established meet the needs of the board and school?

5 *Head of school communications and support*
   - Have we as a board established and maintained a relationship and communication system with the head of school that allows them to do their best work?

- Is the relationship between the board as a whole and the head of school collaborative, respectful, and supportive?
- Does the board (or a board committee) regularly discuss how we support the head of school professionally and personally?

6 *Understanding governance and operations*
- Do we as a board fully understand our role as governors, and are we fulfilling that role?
- Do we as a board hold ourselves accountable to maintaining our fiduciary, generative, and strategic focus?

7 *Goal setting*
- Have we established, and are we actively working to achieve, a set of articulated goals for the school, the head of school, and ourselves as board members?
- Does the board receive regular updates or reports from the administration regarding progress toward strategic plan objectives and goals?
- Does the board engage in a clear process for measuring the achievement of annual goals?

8 *Oversight of finances*
- Do we have the information and resources to fully, proactively, and effectively ensure that the financial position of the school is maintained?
- Are the school's finances reported to the board with a clear and understandable dashboard that provides the needed information?
- Does the board engage regularly (at least annually) in discussions about financial planning

for the future (as opposed to discussions
about current or next year's finances)?

9 *Committees*
   • Do we establish the committees our board
     needs to accomplish its work?
   • Do committees have clearly articulated
     charges and annual goals?
   • Do committees regularly support the preparation
     of board agendas and lead board discussions
     based on their preparation work?

10 *Development and fundraising*
   • Do we as board members actively oversee and
     participate in the school's development
     and fundraising activities?
   • Do we have metrics to evaluate the effectiveness
     of our school's annual fund?
   • Do we know what the expectations are for board
     members regarding development and fundraising?
   • Do we engage in development by regularly reaching
     out to outside people and organizations who
     would benefit and/or support the school?

11 *Board professional development*
   • Do we regularly engage in learning activities that enhance
     our understanding of our roles and responsibilities?
   • Is board orientation sufficient and effective?
   • Is there a board handbook or set of materials
     that provide information about board
     expectations, policies, and procedures?

In addition, there are several areas that can be assessed outside of these practices. These include:

1 *Bylaws* Do our bylaws reflect current practices? Are they accurate? Are the procedures for regularly sharing them with the board effective and followed?

2 *Board handbook* Is it accurate and complete? Does it reflect current practices? Are the procedures for regularly sharing it with the board effective and followed?

3 *Board policies and procedures* Do we have a conflict of interest policy? A board member contract? Investment policy?

4 *Meeting process, agendas, minutes* Do our board process and agendas regularly allow the consideration of strategic and visionary topics? Do we end meetings with specific action steps? Are our minutes sufficiently clear while maintaining appropriate confidentiality?

5 *Strategic plans* Are we currently following an articulated plan? Do we regularly measure the achievement of goals and share these achievements with the wider community?

The work of the board chair is essential to the success of the whole board. Board members, the head of school, and the board chair themself can assess their abilities in several areas, including:

1 *Facilitating meetings* Does the board chair facilitate productive, inclusive, relevant, and outcome-focused meetings?

2 *Supporting the overall achievement of board goals* Does the board chair actively lead the board in taking the steps to achieve goals?

3 *Strategic thinking* Does the board chair actively lead the
   board in thinking strategically on a regular basis?

4 *Supporting the head of school* Does the board
   chair effectively support the professional and
   personal well-being of the head of school?

In addition to assessing the work of the board as a whole, individual board members can and should assess their own, individual efforts. Areas to assess include:

1 *Participation* Do I exercise my duty of care by
   showing up regularly to meetings, fully prepared
   to engage in the work of the board?

2 *Loyalty* Do I consider any potential conflict
   of interest when acting as a board member and
   stay focused on the needs of the school?

3 *Legal awareness* Am I aware of our board's bylaws,
   and do I consider how our practices uphold those
   bylaws as well as other laws and ethics?

4 *Governance focus* Am I confident I understand what is
   expected of me as a board member regarding my governance
   responsibilities? Do I understand the difference between
   governance and operations, where the line is between
   them, and when it should and should not be crossed?

5 *Strategic thinking* Do I endeavor to think strategically as a
   board member and only engage in operational considerations
   when appropriate and invited by the head of school?

6 *Diversity of thought* Do I endeavor to consider topics from
   diverse perspectives, and protect against biased thinking?

7 *Committee work* Do I actively engage in the
   work of one or more committees in order to
   support the work of the board as a whole?

When deciding what to assess, boards benefit from considering their work and achievements in a variety of ways. Moving beyond asking questions about the general work of the board as a whole and being more specific about practices that can be modified and improved will provide a board with data that can be used. Furthermore, asking questions about the work of the board chair and about individual board members' efforts will paint a broader picture of the board that will lead to a more meaningful evaluation of its effectiveness.

HOW AND WHEN TO EVALUATE

A board that gathers and considers all of the assessment data discussed above will have a large amount of data they can use to identify areas for improvement and set future goals. The next step is to evaluate the work of the board. Have you met your expectations? Can you confidently state, based on data, that you have an effective board? While the individual assessment data will provide the information you need to make specific improvements, the overall evaluation of your board will give you the confidence or the impetus to move forward.

Think of an evaluation as a dashboard for your performance: It provides a quick overview of how you are doing. Over time, data-informed dashboards can provide a board with the information they need to set priorities and goals. Boards can choose the method of conveying the evaluation of their performance in whatever manner best supports future growth. A rating scale, similar to one that might be used for classroom performance, can be a useful method for boards to evaluate their overall performance:

- Fully effective/effective/somewhat effective/not effective
- Meets expectations/partially meets expectations/ does not meet expectations

Alternatively, a board may find a summary statement or paragraph describing the performance of the board to be beneficial. However boards decide to convey the information, the performance evaluation provides the basis for the upcoming cycle of board goal setting, focus, and attention over the upcoming year.

"Regular" evaluation will mean different things to different boards. Not all boards will want or need to conduct the full set of assessments listed above each year. Boards should evaluate their performance annually, yet can utilize different sets of assessment data. A board that has not fully assessed all aspects of its work in the recent past may benefit from conducting a full set of assessments for several years as board members learn about themselves and address shortcomings. Boards that have a good sense of their efficacy and focus may be able to administer a smaller set of assessments regularly and only need to conduct a full set of assessments to support their evaluation every two to three years. The key is to identify how the assessment data and evaluation will be used to improve board functioning.

If schools value the contributions of their board members and rely on the governance provided by their boards, they need to ensure that boards are performing at their best. They won't know what their best is, or how well they are performing, if they don't measure that performance. Regular assessment and evaluation need to be a part of the annual process a board engages in as a reflection on their efforts over the past year and a springboard for their forthcoming work.

QUESTIONS TO ASK YOUR BOARD

Do we regularly collect a variety of assessments
to measure our board's efficacy?

Do we evaluate our board and the accomplishment
of its work at the end of each year?

Do we use board assessment data to establish
goals for the upcoming year?

14

———

GOVERNING IN CRISIS

———

There's always an opportunity with crisis. Just as it
forces an individual to look inside himself, it forces a
company to reexamine its policies and practices.

JUDY SMITH

A s I write this, the world remains in a global pandemic
due to COVID-19. To say that schools have operated in
crisis over this past year is an understatement. We have
lived through a series of crises that have pushed educators to the
limits of their cognitive, physical, and emotional endurance. All
schools have had to address how to teach safely, whether remotely
or in-person; many schools dealt with significant enrollment fluctuations; and some had to respond to severe illness and/or death
of a community member from the virus. In the US, an additional
layer has been added with the intensification of the social justice
movement brought about by attacks on and murders of people of
color and other groups. No one could have fully prepared for all
this at once. Nonetheless, those schools that had some sort of crisis

protocols in place, and who had boards that were effective planning and decision-making bodies, fared the best.

A crisis is a challenging, dangerous, or unstable situation that may lead to change that requires difficult decisions to be made. Many things qualify as crises for schools by this definition, such as weather, economic, social, or health events; cyber or physical attacks; reputational declines; and negative social media campaigns. Some of these occur more frequently than others, and we can think of ways to prepare for them if they happen again—which is why we have fire drills in schools. Other events, such as a global pandemic or the economic collapse of 2008 were hard to conceive of, much less predict, before they happened. Nonetheless, a proactive board needs to prepare for all kinds of emergencies and be ready to respond to support their school in any situation. Boards need to ensure that the school administration has a crisis plan for the school community, and they need to have their own board crisis plan to guide them in crisis governance. Alongside the head of school, boards have a critical role to play in managing the stages of a crisis—before, during, and after.

BEFORE THE CRISIS

The best crisis response happens before the event occurs. There are three actions boards can take to prepare for both expected emergencies (things that are more common, such as weather, financial instability, and reputation attacks) and surprises:

1 The first is to be effective and efficient in their everyday
   work, with special attention paid to communication and
   decision-making processes. Boards that have established clear,
   transparent, and regular methods of communicating and
   that have a practiced process for making difficult decisions
   during their meetings (as discussed in Chapter 7) will be

able to apply these skills during a crisis. The most important crisis-planning activity is to be a strategically governing board.

2   The second action a board can take is to think about and plan for the emergency events that are more common. This is hard for many people, as it can trigger emotions from past experiences. However, to enable a school community to most effectively respond in crisis situations, careful planning beforehand is needed. The board can create a list of potential crisis situations and then work with school management to create a board crisis response plan for those situations. How will the board maintain its focus on governance and continue to engage in effective practices as it supports the school during and after a crisis?

3   The third action that a board should take is to consider the more unusual crises that might impact the school, the "black swan" events that could threaten the school's sustainability. This is where generative, "what if" thinking comes into play. Boards should consider questions, such as, "What if a school similar to ours opened a mile away?" "What if our head of school died?" "What if a major subset of our student population (such as international students) could no longer attend our school?" By spending time identifying and thinking about responses to potential crises, boards will be better able to respond if they ever occur.

It is easy to put off crisis planning; there is always something important, and usually something urgent, for boards to consider. Nonetheless, each of these three planning activities is key to full crisis preparation. By spending time in committee and board meetings to address communication and decision-making as they might relate to crisis management, as well as thinking ahead about both routine and "black swan" crises, boards will be better able to support their schools.

DURING THE CRISIS

Unfortunately, the question for a board is not if a crisis will occur—it is when. Situations or events that lead to instability or danger are part of our lives. Boards that have fulfilled their responsibility to plan for these situations will be most effective at crisis management. During the crisis is when plans are put into place. Here are several key elements of a board's responsibilities during a crisis:

1 *Strategic thinking* Using data to inform decisions

2 *Course-correcting* Continually "pivoting" as necessary based on ongoing strategic thinking

3 *Learning* Accessing a variety of opinions and expert advice, regardless of whether it is easy or comfortable

4 *Communication* Ensuring ongoing, comprehensive, and appropriately-timed information-sharing with the head of school and the community

5 *Head of school support* Ensuring that the head of school, who is on the front line of crisis response, has the professional and personal support needed

6 *"Holding space" in the community* Paying attention to the emotional climate of the wider community, being present and accepting of whatever is presented, and responding as needed (Gender and Sexuality Therapy Center 2020)

AFTER THE CRISIS

Once a crisis has been resolved, it is tempting to work quickly to "return to normal" and resume life as it was before the crisis. In some cases, this is possible; in others it is not. In any case, there is critical work for a board to do after the crisis, and to overlook or disregard this post-crisis work is problematic. The first issue is that there may be mental or social health issues that need to be addressed. The second is that there may be significant lessons that can be learned and implemented to improve the school moving forward. The third is that there may be ways the school can better prepare for future crises. It is imperative that boards take the time to consider each of these areas.

Most crises elicit negative emotions in people, and many organizations fail to respond to the mental health of their constituents following an emotional event. When people's sense of safety and/or trust have been damaged, they need time and processing to repair them. Boards can collaborate with the head of school to plan for the mental health needs of the head, administration, faculty and staff, students, and parents following a crisis. This will look different depending on the situation but should be carefully considered in each case.

Engaging in a thorough "post-mortem" discussion following a crisis event is critical for boards so that they may uncover strengths and weaknesses in themselves and their school that can be leveraged and corrected. Boards can look at the causes of the crisis (using root cause analysis will be helpful) to determine if they could have better prepared or mitigated the causes (Motyl 2019). Using that newly developed understanding, boards can determine if there are systems, protocols, or plans that need to be developed to protect from or respond in better ways to future crises.

If you remember the story I told in the introduction of this book, about the water pipes that had a tendency to freeze and cause damage and financial strain on my school, you will see that the prior board in that situation did not take this step after each crisis. They did not consider the cause of the frozen pipes and develop ways to prevent future problems. And so it kept happening. If the board of five years prior to my arrival had established a protocol for discussion after each crisis, my school would have been in a much better position when I arrived.

Boards can and should also consider if there are new understandings that have been uncovered during the crisis. For example, schools (and the world) had to change dramatically during the global COVID-19 pandemic crisis. We had to communicate, conduct business, and teach from a distance. Once we were able to think about returning to some kind of normalcy and begin to engage with one another in person, there was the opportunity to consider if any of the new practices were beneficial in the long run. Boards asked themselves: Will some board meetings be held remotely moving forward? Will this allow for a wider diversity of board members? The opportunities uncovered during a crisis should be highlighted and considered.

Crisis planning is not typically an enjoyable activity. It can trigger past emotions and create anxiety, and involves considering the unknown. And yet it is a key and important responsibility of boards. This work and planning must be ongoing to accommodate and include new board members. Boards that spend the time strategically thinking and planning their response before, during, and after a crisis will fare much better than those without such planning.

QUESTIONS TO ASK YOUR BOARD

Does our board have a crisis plan? If not, how can we develop one?

Does our crisis plan address our activities before, during, and after a crisis?

Does our crisis plan address physical as well as emotional well-being?

Do we regularly review our plan so that all
board members understand it?

GOVERNING WITH CLARITY, STRATEGY & JOY

S erving on an independent school board can and should be a joyful experience. While there will certainly be times of stress, intensity, crisis, and even conflict—as there are in every other aspect of life—board service does not need to be an unpleasant or self-less endeavor. There are numerous rewards. For many, serving on an independent school board is a source of rich personal and professional connection. Board service is an opportunity to learn about systems, education, and organizations. It is also an opportunity to learn about decision making, strategy, critical thinking, and conflict resolution. And board service is service, allowing us to contribute in meaningful ways to our community.

In a recent conversation with a head of school who supports her own board and serves on the board of another independent school,

201

she said, "I find board work to be an antidote to the sometimes depressing circumstances of everyday life. It is so fundamental for a board to be forward-thinking in a world where our sphere of concern is large and can feel out of control. Boards bring us to a world of influence where you can have an impact; where your thoughts, beliefs, and opinions matter. I have always thought of this as honorable work, and it is practice for what we can expect from society" (Lise Charlier, personal conversation 2021).

When board members have clarity about their roles and responsibilities and understand the nature of governance and its application, it allows them to be confident in their work. When boards pay attention to and intentionally facilitate a culture and climate that allows for diversity of thought and perspective, and that fosters inclusive participation, the power of board members' contributions can be fully realized. And when boards practice strategic thinking on a regular, consistent basis, carefully considering *all* that they do through data and perspective-informed lenses, they will be satisfied that they are impacting the outcomes that allow their schools to thrive. Confidence, clarity, professional growth, personal connection, and satisfaction are some of the many rewards that small school board members experience as a result of engaging in strategic governance.

ACKNOWLEDGMENTS

———

This book would not have come to fruition had I not responded to a listserv post about a publishing webinar hosted by Emily Barrosse in the fall of 2020. I have had several ideas for books floating around in my head for a while, yet never had the focus, drive, or discipline to sit down and put any of them on paper. Actually, I think negative self-talk and lack of confidence were the main reasons I hadn't done much writing. Yet over the past few years I've been working on clearing out those limiting voices in my head, and Emily's workshop came at a time when I was feeling strong and optimistic. In her webinar, she promoted a writing group for women, and the first meeting was in two days. I signed up immediately. Emily's warmth, support, and practicality, along with the camaraderie and encouragement from the women in the writing group (whom I now call friends), have propelled me to write this book. Thanks, Emily B, Kathryn, Emily V-B, Sara, Louisa, Annie, Jenny, Patsy, and Katherine—I am so grateful the universe put you in my life!

From the initial workshop with Emily Barrosse, I was fortunate enough to be able to publish this book through her newly established publishing house for women authors, Bold Story Press. I am deeply grateful for the time, attention, thoughtfulness, and honesty of Karen Gulliver whose editing genius has made this work so much better; Julianna Scott Fein, the production manager who kept us all on schedule; Karen Polaski, whose design genius made it look so good; Esther Reisberg, whose detail-oriented proofreading cleaned up the manuscript; and Emily, of course, who cheered us on and made it all possible. Thanks for such a smooth introduction to the world of book publishing!

I am deeply indebted to the friends and colleagues who took the time to read, edit, and give me feedback on this manuscript. Your expertise and insightfulness has made it a much better, more honest, and well-rounded book. Thanks to Peter Baily, Norm Colb, Liz Dover, Michelle Parker, Roger Smith, and Val Wise. You are some of the smartest people I know, and, more importantly, great friends!

Ginny McDonald was the board chair at Seneca Academy for most of the time I was head of school. Her wisdom, level-headedness, kindness, and insight were invaluable to me and to the school. I learned a tremendous amount from her about governance and leadership. I am forever grateful.

I am extremely fortunate to have a circle of women who serve as sounding boards, mentors, and coaches as well as friends. I am deeply indebted to the love, support, and wisdom from Aubrey Bursch, Tara Claeys, Jen Cort, Cheryl Crim, Angie Dalton, Julie Eagle, Jean Gearon, Jill Goodman, Bela Meghani, and Val Wise. And I am grateful for the love, support, and friendship of my beloved sisters, Linda and Mariana.

To my greatest cheerleader: Brian. You have never ceased to believe in me and have encouraged me to reach for the stars even when they seemed outrageously unattainable. I am grateful for your partnership and excited to share our successes as we continue on this journey together.

BOARD EXPERTISE
SELF-REPORT FORM

NAME

Please circle all of the identifiers, skills, abilities,
and characteristics that apply to you.

GENDER
Male
Female
Nonbinary

AGE
21–35   36–50
51–65   Over 65

RACE / ETHNICITY
African American
American Indian/Alaskan Native
Asian or Pacific Islander
White
Latino/Hispanic
Middle Eastern

CONSTITUENCY
Parent
Past Parent
Grandparent
Alumna/us
Funder
Local Community Member
Local Business Owner/Member

ADDITIONAL CHARACTERISTICS
Ability to raise the
   school's image
Ability to refer students
Ability to raise money

CURRENT PROFESSION	AREA OF EXPERTISE
Accounting	Accounting
Advancement	Administration/General
Arts	Child Development
Banking	Community Involvement
Business Owner	Development
Civil Service	Education
Corporate	Facilities Maintenance
Education: Elementary	Facilities Management
Education: Secondary	Faculty Concerns
Education: Higher Education	Financial Management
Electrician	Financial Projection
Entrepreneur	Fundraising
Finance /Investments	Head of School
Human Relations	Health Care
Information Systems and Tech	Human Resources
Insurance	Information Services/ Technology
Law	Investments
Marketing	Leadership
Media	Legal Affairs
Medicine	Marketing
Nonprofit	Media/Public Relations
Organization Leader	Nonprofit Governance
Politics	Personnel Management
Real Estate	School Parent
Religion	Strategic Planning
Social Services	Teaching
Teacher	

SAMPLE BOARD EXPERTISE SUMMARY SPREADSHEET

	Deepika Mehta	John Davies	Yi-Wen Song	Kwame Darko	Ayianna Jones	Ben Lee	Aryani Ong	Rodney Hines	TOTALS
GENDER									
Male									
Female									
Nonbinary									
AGE									
21–35									
36–50									
51–65									
Over 65									
RACE/ETHNICITY									
African American									
American Indian/Alaskan Native									
Asian or Pacific Islander									
White									
Latino/Hispanic									
MIddle Eastern									
Etc.									

PROFESSION	Deepika Mehta	John Davies	Yi-Wen Song	Kwame Darko	Ayianna Jones	Ben Lee	Aryani Ong	Rodney Hines	TOTALS
Accounting									
Advancement									
Arts									
Banking									
Business Owner									
Civil Service									
Etc.									
AREA OF EXPERTISE									
Accounting									
Administration /General									
Child Development									
Community Involvement									
Development									
Education									
Facilities Management									
Etc.									
CONSTITUENCY									
Parent									
Past Parent									
Grandparent									
Alumna/us									
Etc.									
ADDITIONAL CHARACTERISTICS									
Ability to Raise Image									
Ability to Refer Students									
Ability to Raise Money									
Other									

THE XYZ SCHOOL'S
BOARD MEMBER CONTRACT

As a member of the XYZ School's board, I have a legal and ethical responsibility to ensure that the organization does the best work possible in pursuit of its goals. I support the purpose and mission of the organization and pledge my commitment to assist in carrying out its work.

As a board member, I will consistently act responsibly and prudently. I understand my duties to include:

1   Legal, fiscal and moral responsibility, along with my fellow board members, for the well-being of this organization. As such, it is my responsibility to
    • Know and approve all policies and programs and oversee their implementation
    • Take responsibility for making decisions on organization issues and board matters
    • Interpret the organization's work and values to the community, represent the organization as appropriate
    • Keep up-to-date on the business of the organization
    • Be familiar with our budget and take an active part in the budget-planning process
    • Excuse myself from discussions, decisions, and votes where I may have a conflict of interest

2 Attendance at _____ board meetings per year and an annual board
   retreat. Additionally, I will serve on at least one board committee.

3 An annual personal financial contribution to the organization at
   a level that is meaningful for me. This may be given as a one-
   time donation each year or as installments during the course
   of the year [or insert minimum donation amount expected].

4 Active participation in one or more fundraising
   activities. This may include individual and/or
   special event solicitation or direct appeals.

5 Working in good faith with my fellow board members and
   staff toward the achievement of the organization's goals.

Should I fail to fulfill these commitments to the organization, I
understand that a member of the board leadership will call upon me
to discuss my responsibilities. Should there come a time where I am
no longer able to fulfill my obligations to the organization, it will be
my responsibility to resign my position as a member of the board.

As a board member, I understand that the organization will be responsible to me in the following ways:

1 I will be sent, without request, financial reports and an update of
   organizational activities that allow me to meet the duty of care
   standards of the law. Further, I expect that I will have information
   about programs and policies, goals and objectives as appropriate.

2 Opportunities will be provided for me to discuss with
   the head of school and the board president/chair the
   organization's programs, goals, activities and status.

3 It is expected that board members and the head of school
   will respond in a straightforward fashion to questions
   that I feel are necessary to carry out my fiscal, legal,
   and moral responsibilities to the organization.

4 Board members and the head of school will work in good
   faith with me toward achievement of our goals.

5 If the organization does not fulfill its commitments to me, I
   may call upon the board president/chair and head of school
   to discuss the organization's responsibilities to me.

6 The organization will carry directors' and officers' liability insurance.

BOARD MEMBER'S TERM

PRINT BOARD MEMBER NAME

BOARD MEMBER SIGNATURE

DATE

PRINT BOARD PRESIDENT/CHAIR NAME

BOARD PRESIDENT/CHAIR SIGNATURE

DATE

REFERENCES

Baker, Troy, Stephen Campbell and David Ostroff. 2015.
Independent School Leadership: Heads, Boards, and Strategic Thinking. Peabody Journal of Education, 91:5, 574–587,
DOI: 10.1080/0161956X.2016.1227165

Barlow, Jeremy. 2016. "Nonprofit Board Legal Responsibilities."
BoardEffect. https://www.boardeffect.com/blog/non-profit
-board-legal-responsibilities/

The Belonging Project at Stanford. n.d. Accessed May 14, 2021. https:
//med.stanford.edu/psychiatry/special-initiatives/belonging.html

Biddle, Bruce and David Berliner. 2002. "Small Class Size and Its
Effects." *Educational Leadership* v59 n5: p12–23.

Birk, Matthias. 2020. "Why Leaders Need Meditation Now More
Than Ever." HBR, March 22.

Bloom, Howard and Rebecca Unterman. 2014. "Can Small
High Schools of Choice Improve Educational Prospects
for Disadvantaged Students?" *Journal of Policy Analysis and
Management*, Vol. 33, No. 2, 290–319.

BoardSource. 2017. "Executive Committee." Accessed April 16,
2021. https://boardsource.org/resources/executive-committee/

BoardSource. 2021. *Leading with Intent: BoardSource Index of Nonprofit Board Practices*. Washington, D.C. https://leadingwithintent.org/

Broughman, Stephen P., Brian Kincel, Jennifer Willinger, and Jennifer Peterson. 2021. *Characteristics of Private Schools in the United States: Results from the 2019–20 Private School Universe Survey*. The National Center for Education Statistics at IES; US Department of Education.

Brower, Tracy. 2021. "Missing Your People: Why Belonging Is So Important and How to Create It." *Forbes* January 10. https://www.forbes.com/sites/tracybrower/2021/01/10/missing-your-people-why-belonging-is-so-important-and-how-to-create-it/?sh=74b21bac7c43

Carr, Evan, Andrew Reece, Gabriella Rosen Kellerman, and Alexi Robichaux. 2019. "The Value of Belonging at Work." *Harvard Business Review* Dec. 16. https://hbr.org/2019/12/the-value-of-belonging-at-work

Carver, John. 2006. *Boards That Make a Difference: A New Design for Leadership in Nonprofit and Public Organizations*. San Francisco: Jossey-Bass, 3rd edition.

Chait, Richard, William Ryan, and Barbara Taylor. 2005. *Governance as Leadership: Reframing the Work of Nonprofit Boards*. Hoboken, NJ: John Wiley & Sons.

Chowdhury, Madhuleena Roy. 2021. "The Science and Psychology of Goal-Setting 101." *Positive Psychology.com* June 15. https://positivepsychology.com/goal-setting-psychology/

Colb, Norman. 2011. "The Board of Trustees—Friend, Foe, Boss, or Partner?" In *The Head's Handbook: A Guide for Aspiring, New, and Experienced Heads of School*, edited by Gene Batiste and Jay Riven, 189–200. USA: NAIS.

Cotton, Kathleen. 1996. *School Size, School Climate, and Student Performance*. Portland, OR: NWREL, Close Up #2.

The DeBono Group. n.d. "Six Thinking Hats." Accessed June 28, 2021. https://www.debonogroup.com/services/core-programs /six-thinking-hats/

DeKuyper, Mary Hundley. 2007. Trustee Handbook: *A Guide to Effective Governance for Independent School Boards* 9th Edition. USA: NAIS.

Farr, Elizabeth Kolb. 2021. "The Importance of Fundraising Strategy." *NAIS Independent School Magazine*. Spring. https:// www.nais.org/magazine/independent-school/spring-2021 /the-importance-of-fundraising-strategy/

Fussell, Chris. 2015. "The Biggest Career Lesson This Navy SEAL Learned in Iraq." *Fortune* June 21. https://fortune.com/2015 /06/21/chris-fussell-productivity-at-work/

Gender and Sexuality Therapy Center. 2020. "What 'Holding Space' Means + 5 Tips to Practice." January 17. https://gstherapycenter .com/blog/2020/1/16/what-holding-space-means-5-tips-to-practice#

Grauer, Stuart. 2014. "Q&A with Stuart Grauer." *Alternative Education Resource Organization* http://www .educationrevolution.org/store/qa-with-stuart-grauer/

Gurteen, David. n.d. "The Influence of Group Size on Conversation: More Than Five people and It Is Not a Conversation." In *Conversational Leadership*. Accessed June 28, 2021. https://conversational-leadership.net/optimal-group-size/

Hak, Andrea. 2019. "Why Diverse Teams Make Better Business Decisions." *TNW News*. https://thenextweb.com/news/why -diverse-teams-make-better-business-decisions

Hamzelou, Jessica. 2017. Your Autopilot Mode Is Real—Now We Know How the Brain Does It. New Scientist, October, 23.

Harvard Business Review. 2019. *HBR Guide to Thinking Strategically.* Boston, Massachusetts: Harvard Business Review Press.

Hayes, Kate. 2017. "A Roadmap to Better Boards." *Stanford Social Innovation Review.* https://ssir.org/articles/entry /a_roadmap_to_better_boards

Horwath, Rich. 2020. "The Origin of Strategy." *Strategic Thinking Institute* (Blog) July, 1. https://www.strategyskills.com/the -origin-of-strategy/

Independent School Management. 2019. *Better Boards, Better Schools, The ISM Guide for Private School Trusteeship and Strategic Governance.* Wilmington, DE: Independent School Management.

Internal Revenue Service. n.d. "Governance and Related Topics - 501(c)(3) Organizations." Accessed April 28, 2021. https://www .irs.gov/pub/irs-tege/governance_practices.pdf

Keping, Yu. 2017. "Governance and Good Governance: A New Framework for Political Analysis." *Fudan Journal of the Humanities and Social Sciences* 1-8. 10.1007/s40647-017-0197-4.

Kuziemko, Ilyana. 2006. "Using Shocks to School Enrollment to Estimate the Effect of School Size on Student Achievement." *Economics of Education Review* 25.1: 25, 1, 63–75.

Larson, Erik. 2017. "New Research: Diversity + Inclusion = Better Decision Making at Work." *Forbes.* https://www.forbes.com /sites/eriklarson/2017/09/21/new-research-diversity-inclusion -better-decision-making-at-work/?sh=132ff6d14cbf

Lewis, John. 2020. "Building a Better Dashboard for School Financial Health." *NAIS Independent School Magazine*, Winter. https: //www.nais.org/magazine/independent-school/winter-2020 /building-a-better-dashboard-for-school-financial-health/

Maraboli, Steve. 2009. *Life, The Truth, and Being Free.* Port Washington, NY: A Better Today Publishing.

Mathis, William. 2016. "The Effectiveness of Class Size Reduction." *National Education Policy Center.* https://nepc.colorado.edu /publication/research-based-options

Michalski, Camilla A., Lori M. Diemert, John F. Helliwell, Vivek Goel, and Laura C. Rosella. 2020.

"Relationship between Sense of Community Belonging and Self-rated Health across Life Stages." *SSM - Population Health* Volume 12, 100676.

Moats, Maria Castañón, Paul DiNicola, and Leah Malone. 2021. "Four Common Biases in Boardroom Culture." In *Strategy + Business: Leadership.* Autumn 2021 / Issue 104. https://www .strategy-business.com/article/Four-common-biases-in -boardroom-culture

Motyl, Pawel. 2019. *Labyrinth: The Art of Decision-Making.* Vancouver, BC: Page Two Books.

NAIS. 2011. *The Trustee Dashboard.* NAIS.org. https://www.nais .org/getmedia/de6be128-1ae6-4829-ae2d-1cd018b880fb/NAIS _Trustee_Dashboard_for_PDF.pdf

NAIS. 2018. *2018 NAIS Governance Study.* NAIS.org. https://www .nais.org/articles/pages/research/2018-nais-governance-study/

National Center for Education Statistics. n.d. "School Choice in the United States: 2019." Accessed September 15, 2021. https://nces .ed.gov/programs/schoolchoice/ind_03.asp

National Center for Education Statistics. n.d. "School Choice in the United States: 2019." Accessed May 24, 2021. https://nces .ed.gov/programs/schoolchoice/index.asp

National Small Schools Conference. n.d. "About." Accessed May 23, 2021. https://www.nationalsmallschoolsconference.org/about

Parker, Priya. 2018. *The Art of Gathering: How We Meet and Why It Matters.* UK: Penguin Random House.

The Pew Fund for Health and Human Services. 2007. *Governance as Leadership: Reframing the Work of the Nonprofit Board.* Seminar led by William Ryan, October 29, 2007.

Riople, Leslie. 2021. "The Importance, Benefits, and Value of Goal Setting." *Positive Psychology.com* April 16. https://positivepsychology.com/benefits-goal-setting/

Rogen, Stephanie. 2018. *Creating Schools That Thrive: A Blueprint for Strategy.* Greenwich, CT: Stephanie Rogen, Greenwich Leadership Partners.

Romero, Carissa. 2015. *What We Know About Belonging from Scientific Research.* Mindset Scholars Network, Stanford University.

Ross, Nancy. 2002. "Community Belonging and Health." *Health Rep.* 13(3):33–9.

Rupprecht, Silke, Pia Falke, Niko Kohls, Chris Tamdjidi, Marc Wittmann, and Wendy Kersemaekers. 2019. "Mindful Leader Development: How Leaders Experience the Effects of Mindfulness Training on Leader Capabilities." *Frontiers in Psychology,* May 15.

Small Schools Coalition. n.d. "About the SSC." Accessed May 15, 2021. https://smallschoolscoalition.org/about/

Torres, Amanda. 2019. Research Insights: Why Parents Choose Independent Schools. *NAIS Independent School Magazine,* Winter.

Trower, Cathy. 2013. *The Practitioners Guide to Governance as Leadership: Building High-Performing Nonprofit Boards.* San Francisco: Jossey-Bass.

Zimmerman, Kim Ann. 2017. "What Is Culture?" *Livescience.* July 12.

ABOUT
BOLD STORY PRESS

―――

Bold Story Press is a curated, woman-owned hybrid publishing company with a mission of publishing well-written stories by women. If your book is chosen for publication, our team of expert editors and designers will work with you to publish a professionally edited and designed book. Every woman has a story to tell. If you have written yours and want to explore publishing with Bold Story Press, contact us at https://boldstorypress.com.

**BOLD
STORY
PRESS**

The Bold Story Press logo, designed by Grace Arsenault, was inspired by the nom de plume, or pen name, a sad necessity at one time for female authors who wanted to publish. The woman's face hidden in the quill is the profile of Virginia Woolf, who, in addition to being an early feminist writer, founded and ran her own publishing company, Hogarth Press.

Made in the USA
Monee, IL
23 May 2022

96906597R00134